Rock and Roll

EXAMINING POP CULTURE

LAURA K. EGENDORF
Book Editor

Daniel Leone,
President

Bonnie Szumski,
Publisher

Scott Barbour,
Managing Editor

James D. Torr,
Series Editor

Greenhaven Press, Inc.
San Diego, California

Every effort has been made to trace the owners of copyrighted material. The articles in this volume may have been edited for content, length, and/or reading level. The titles have been changed to enhance the editorial purpose.

No part of this book may be reproduced or used in any form or by any means, electrical, mechanical, or otherwise, including, but not limited to, photocopy, recording, or any information storage and retrieval system, without prior written permission from the publisher.

Library of Congress Cataloging-in-Publication Data

Rock and roll / Laura K. Egendorf, book editor.
p. cm.—(Examining pop culture)
Includes bibliographical references and index.
ISBN 0-7377-0862-X (pbk. : alk. paper) —
ISBN 0-7377-0863-8 (hc. : alk. paper) —
1. Rock music—Social aspects. 2. Rock music—Political aspects.
I. Egendorf, Laura K., 1973–   II. Series.

ML3918.R63 R63   2002
781.66—dc21
                                                              2001045255
                                                              CIP

Cover Photo: © Lynn Goldsmith/Corbis

© 2002 by Greenhaven Press, Inc.
PO Box 28909, San Diego, CA 92198–0990

Printed in the U.S.A.

CONTENTS

influenced the Beatles' early music. However, the Beatles eventually developed their own unique sound and pioneered a new style of British rock.

Chapter 2: The Politics of Rock

Chapter 3: The Dangers of Rock and Roll

Chapter 4: The Future of Rock and Roll

distribution of rock and roll. The Internet is not able to promote music as well as the major labels.

FOREWORD

POPULAR CULTURE IS THE COMMON SET OF ARTS, entertainments, customs, beliefs, and values shared by large segments of society. Russel B. Nye, one of the founders of the study of popular culture, wrote that "not until the appearance of mass society in the eighteenth century could popular culture, as one now uses the term, be said to exist." According to Nye, the Industrial Revolution and the rise of democracy in the eighteenth and nineteenth centuries led to increased urbanization and the emergence of a powerful middle class. In nineteenth-century Europe and North America, these trends created audiences for the popular arts that were larger, more concentrated, and more well off than at any point in history. As a result, more people shared a common culture than ever before.

The technological advancements of the twentieth century vastly accelerated the spread of popular culture. With each new advance in mass communication—motion pictures, radio, television, and the Internet—popular culture has become an increasingly pervasive aspect of everyday life.

Popular entertainment—in the form of movies, television, theater, music recordings and concerts, books, magazines, sporting events, video games, restaurants, casinos, theme parks, and other attractions—is one very recognizable aspect of popular culture. In his 1999 book *The Entertainment Economy: How Mega-Media Forces Are Transforming Our Lives*, Michael J. Wolf argues that entertainment is becoming the dominant feature of American society: "In choosing where we buy French fries, how we relate to political candidates, what airline we want to fly, what pajamas we choose for our kids, and which mall we want to buy them in, entertainment is increasingly influencing every one of those choices. . . . Multiply that by the billions of choices that, collectively, all of us make each day and you have a portrait of a society in which entertainment is one of its leading institutions."

It is partly this pervasive quality of popular culture that makes it worthy of study. James Combs, the author of *Polpop: Politics and Popular Culture in America*, explains that examining popular culture is important because it can shape people's attitudes and beliefs:

> Popular culture is so much a part of our lives that we cannot deny its developmental powers. . . . Like formal education or family rearing, popular culture is part of our "learning environment.". . . Though our pop culture education is informal—we usually do not attend to pop culture for its "educational" value—it nevertheless provides us with information and images upon which we develop our opinions and attitudes. We would not be what we are, nor would our society be quite the same, without the impact of popular culture.

Examining popular culture is also important because popular movies, music, fads, and the like often reflect popular opinions and attitudes. Christopher D. Geist and Jack Nachbar explain in *The Popular Culture Reader*, "the popular arts provide a gauge by which we can learn what Americans are thinking, their fears, fantasies, dreams, and dominant mythologies. The popular arts reflect the values of the multitude."

This two-way relationship between popular culture and society is evident in many modern discussions of popular culture. Does the glorification of guns by many rap artists, for example, merely reflect the realities of inner-city life, or does it also contribute to the problem of gun violence? Such questions also arise in discussions of the popular culture of the past. Did the Vietnam protest music of the late 1960s and early 1970s, for instance, simply reflect popular antiwar sentiments, or did it help turn public opinion against the war? Examining such questions is an important part of understanding history.

Greenhaven Press's Examining Pop Culture series provides students with the resources to begin exploring these questions. Each volume in the series focuses on a particular aspect of popular culture, with topics as varied as popular culture itself. Books in the series may focus on a particular genre, such as *Rap and Hip Hop*, while others may cover a specific medium, such as *Computers and the Internet*. Volumes such as *Body Piercing and Tattoos* have their focus on recent trends in popular culture, while titles like *Americans' Views About War* have a broader historical scope.

In each volume, an introductory essay provides a general

overview of the topic. The selections that follow offer a survey of critical thought about the subject. The readings in *Americans' Views About War*, for example, are arranged chronologically: Essays explore how popular films, songs, television programs, and even comic books both reflected and shaped public opinion about American wars from World War I through Vietnam. The essays in *Violence in Film and TV*, on the other hand, take a more varied approach: Some provide historical background, while others examine specific genres of violent film, such as horror, and still others discuss the current controversy surrounding the issue.

Each book in the series contains a comprehensive index to help readers quickly locate material of interest. Perhaps most importantly, each volume has an annotated bibliography to aid interested students in conducting further research on the topic. In today's culture, what is "popular" changes rapidly from year to year and even month to month. Those who study popular culture must constantly struggle to keep up. The volumes in Greenhaven's Examining Pop Culture series are intended to introduce readers to the major themes and issues associated with each topic, so they can begin examining for themselves what impact popular culture has on their own lives.

INTRODUCTION

IN 2000, A TOTAL OF $14.3 BILLION WAS SPENT ON music recordings in the United States. Of those purchases, the most popular genre was rock music, which constituted almost one-fourth of the market. For almost fifty years, rock and roll has been a predominant musical style in the United States and much of the world. Yet despite its popularity, rock music remains in many ways the music of the marginalized. Many of its greatest artists have been those who have been left on the outskirts of society because of their race, gender, class, or sexuality. Throughout its inception, and into modern times, the link between rock music and society's outsiders has led to negative reactions from certain segments of mainstream society.

The Beginnings of Rock and Roll

In the 1950s, during the earliest days of rock and roll, the most influential musicians were those who had the least power in American society: African Americans. The music that they developed in the first half of the twentieth century laid the groundwork for rock and roll. In the 1920s and 1930s, for example, Robert Johnson and other musicians made blues an important musical style. Johnson was an especially influential guitarist; according to lore, he had sold his soul to the devil in exchange for guitar skills. A type of piano-based blues music known as "boogie" also gained considerable popularity following World War II. Rhythm and blues—the precursor to rock—was also popular, but until the early 1950s, those songs were only played on African American radio stations and sold in African American stores.

The influences on rock and roll were not exclusively African American, however. Rock critic Simon Frith writes in *Sound Effects* that country music, which was created largely by southern whites, shared several parallels to the blues in terms of the vocal and instrumental techniques. However, country music was much more conservative in the themes of its lyrics.

Eventually an increasing number of white deejays, most notably Cleveland's Alan Freed, began to play R&B, which

Freed redubbed "rock and roll." That term was not new. According to Charlie Gillett, in his seminal book on the early years of rock and roll, *The Sound of the City*, the term had already been used in blues songs to refer to sexual intercourse and dancing.

Elvis Presley

Perhaps the four most important rock and roll singers of the 1950s were Elvis Presley, Jerry Lee Lewis, Chuck Berry, and Little Richard. The first two men were poor white southerners. The latter two were African American and, in Richard Penniman's case, homosexual. Chuck Berry became the first guitar hero of the rock era, making full use of the electric guitar that had been first designed in the 1930s and perfected by Les Paul and Leo Fender in the 1940s and 1950s. Richard and Lewis were known for their piano playing and frenetic performances. But it was Elvis who best combined all of rock's early influences; his music developed from the combination of country, blues, and gospel that came from growing up in Mississippi. In his cornerstone work *Mystery Train*, rock critic Greil Marcus writes of Elvis: "No singer emerged with anything like Elvis's combination of great talent and conscious ambition, and there is no way a new American hero could have gotten out of the South and to the top . . . without that combination."

Elvis might have reached the top in the mid-1950s, but his rise was not met with universal acceptance. According to Linda Martin and Kerry Segrave, the authors of *Anti-Rock: The Opposition to Rock 'n' Roll*, many adults considered rock and roll to be a threat because of its origins in African American music and because it symbolized the freedom of irresponsible adolescence. They write: "From the beginning rock and roll was viewed by the adult world as the clarion call to teenagers to rise up and defy their adult elders, to flaunt their morality, to mock their ideals, to break away from adult control, to reject the adult world." Trent Hill notes in his essay "The Enemy Within: Censorship in Rock Music in the 1950s" that white middle-class parents feared the influence of African American music on their children and believed the beats and lyrics could encourage promiscuity. Rock concerts were considered riotous, though as Martin and Segrave argue, such a term was often exaggerated. According to them: "Most of these incidents just involved kids dancing in the aisles at theaters; jiving in their seats; and stomping, clapping, and yelling a lot—having a good time, in short."

The musician who attracted the most negative attention, perhaps not surprisingly, was Elvis Presley. His stage demeanor, which was marked by pelvic gyrations and bumps and grinds, was viewed disdainfully by many authority figures. When he appeared on the *Ed Sullivan Show*, Presley was filmed only from the waist up. Some radio stations banned the playing of Presley's records. This distaste for Presley continued until 1958, when he was drafted into the army.

The Birth of Folk Rock

By the early 1960s, the stars of rock's first half-decade had faded from the scene. Elvis had been in Germany, serving in the army; when he returned, his singing career was limited to the songs he recorded for his movies. Chuck Berry and Jerry Lee Lewis faced legal problems that lessened their popularity; Buddy Holly died in a plane crash; and Little Richard left rock music for the ministry. In their place was a series of interchangeable "teen idols"—including Fabian, Bobby Rydell, and Frankie Avalon—that presented little threat to adult society. By this point it seemed that rock and roll had faded away. Gillett writes: "By the time these singers had become the most regular hit makers in America, authentic rock 'n' roll had already become a distant memory."

That situation continued until 1963, when two important trends began to emerge—folk music and the British Invasion. These music styles brought to the scene several of the most important artists of rock history, most notably the Beatles, Bob Dylan, and the Rolling Stones. Responding to the political and social issues of their time, these musicians saved rock and roll from an early death and once again placed the music on the side of the disenfranchised.

In the 1930s, folk music had become a way to express radical political ideas. The audience of these songs was urban and educated, in contrast to the rural workers who were the subjects of the lyrics. When political activism became popular again in the 1960s, folk music reemerged. These songwriters, who were predominantly white middle-class males, expressed support for African Americans, women, and the working class and criticized America's decision to enter Vietnam. Among the most famous of these songs were Dylan's "The Times They Are A-Changing," Phil Ochs's "I Ain't Marching Anymore," and Pete Seeger's rendition of the civil rights anthem "We Shall Overcome."

Folk music changed dramatically on July 25, 1965, when Dylan performed with an electric guitar at the Newport Folk Festival. With this new electric sound, folk music was transformed into folk rock and made popular by Dylan and the Byrds, among others. Folk rock also became an important form for women musicians, with the advent of the careers of Joan Baez and Judy Collins. The folk music scene culminated in 1969 at the Woodstock Festival. Among the musicians who performed at the three-day concert were folk artists such as Baez, Arlo Guthrie, Ritchie Havens, and Crosby, Stills, Nash, and Young.

The British Invasion

Yet the change in rock music was not on American soil alone. Almost from its beginning, rock and roll had been the favorite music of British working-class teenagers. According to Peter Wicke, the director of the Centre for Popular Music Research at the Humboldt University in Berlin, American rock music also gave British youth a way to develop their own culture apart from the conservative society in which they lived. Among these youth were three young men from Liverpool— John Lennon, Paul McCartney, and George Harrison. After several lineup changes, they settled on a drummer named Richard Starkey, known more commonly as Ringo Starr, and thus the Beatles were born. The Beatles and their peers—the Who, the Kinks, the Rolling Stones, and other acts—brought a uniquely British type of music to the world. Just as Elvis and Chuck Berry had presented the concerns of American adolescents in their songs, the British musicians expressed the views of English postwar working-class society.

Although the popularity of the Beatles began in Britain, it soon spread to America. By the time the quartet performed on the *Ed Sullivan Show* in January 1964, Beatlemania had swept the nation. Yet like Elvis nearly a decade before, there were some who considered their appearance threatening—their hairstyles, for example, were decried as too long. The Beatles lost considerable popularity after John Lennon's declaration in 1966 that they were "more popular than Jesus." And the Beatles were hardly seen as the most dangerous of the British Invasion bands. The brothers who led the Kinks got into violent arguments; the Who smashed instruments on stage and had a lead singer who mimicked the stuttering of methamphetamine addicts in their first big hit, "My Generation"; the Stones exuded a general air of danger, which was exploited by their manager Andrew Oldham in his press campaign, "Would You Let Your Daughter Marry a Rolling Stone?"

As had been the case a decade earlier, rock was subject to censorship in the 1960s. Once again, the *Ed Sullivan Show* tried to control the way rock bands appeared. The Doors and the Stones were told to change the lyrics to their respective hits, "Light My Fire" and "Let's Spend the Night Together." The Stones complied but the Doors did not. Songs by those bands and other popular groups were also censored by their record companies and radio stations or banned outright.

The Birth of Heavy Metal

As the 1960s progressed, the music gradually became edgier; the harmonies of the Beach Boys and the Beatles fell by the wayside. When heavy metal began in the late 1960s, youth culture had lost much of its optimism. In her examination of heavy metal, *Heavy Metal: A Cultural Sociology*, Deena Weinstein writes:

> The Woodstock triumph of August 1969 was negated by the horror of Altamont [a festival headlined by the Rolling Stones in which the Hell's Angels, who were hired as security, killed an audience member] in December of that same year. The breakup of the Beatles in 1970 marked the end of a group that had in many ways symbolized the youth culture. Heavy metal was born amidst the ashes of the failed youth revolution.

The development of heavy metal had begun several years earlier. The genre was influenced by the Yardbirds, Cream, and other British blues-rock bands of the 1960s, whose music centered around a distorted guitar sound, a powerful rhythm section, and screaming vocals. In fact, after the Yardbirds broke up, their lead guitarist Jimmy Page went on to form the first important heavy metal band, Led Zeppelin.

Heavy metal is one of the most controversial rock genres. By the 1980s, the emphasis in the lyrics on male sexual prowess and the dark side of life led to fears of the influence of heavy metal on adolescents. One organization that was particularly concerned was the Parents Music Resource Coalition. Founded in 1985 by wives of Washington powerbrokers, including Tipper Gore, wife of then–Tennessee senator Albert Gore Jr., the PMRC held hearings on the effects of lyrics of popular music. While not all the bands targeted were heavy metal, acts such as Twisted Sister and WASP were accused of recording songs that were inappropriate for children. In addition, Judas Priest, Ozzy Osbourne, AC/DC, and other artists have been accused by parents, supporters of the PMRC, and conservative organizations of encouraging their fans to commit suicide and murder. Judas Priest, for example, was sued by two sets of parents who alleged that their sons' suicides were prompted by subliminal messages in the song "Better By You Better Than Me." The judge ruled in favor of the band.

Punk Rock: Anarchy in the U.K. and U.S.A.

Around the same time that heavy metal was first beginning, a new style of music was also starting in the United States, although it would not make its full impact until the mid-to-late 1970s.

The punk movement began in the late 1960s and was led by Velvet Underground, whose lyrics dealt with hard drugs and other taboo subjects and whose music featured heavy drums, loud guitar, and tuneless singing. MC5 and the Stooges also exhibited these musical qualities; MC5's lyrics were also often political in nature. However, it was not until the 1970s that a true American punk scene was born. Its origins were in New York City, in particular the club CBGB's. The band most associated with the New York sound was the Ramones. *New York Times* music writer Jon Pareles describes the Ramones' sound: "With just three or four chords, concise melodies, loud guitars and fast tempos, the Ramones' two-minute songs distilled the simple thrills of pre-psychedelic rock 'n' roll." Their simple and repetitive lyrics focused on outsiders—the mentally ill, drug users, disaffected adolescents, and punk rockers themselves.

The music of the Ramones and the others inspired youth on the other side of the Atlantic. When punk rock developed in England, the country was facing severe economic problems that particularly affected its lower-class youth. English youth who dropped out of school had trouble finding jobs; in 1977, almost 30 percent of the under-eighteen population was unemployed. Inflation was high and strikes were common. These youth felt like outsiders because of their inability to participate in the British economy, and many of them joined the punk subculture as a way of expressing their status in society. Peter Wicke contends: "Unemployment always means social isolation, being shut out from other people's normal everyday life, which for the punks led to a marked consciousness of the division between 'us' and 'them', expressed in a form of self-presentation which made the contrast quite visible." Punk rockers dyed their hair in unnatural colors, put safety pins through their lips and ears, wore clothes made of leather and rubber that were associated with bondage and fetishism.

It was the content of the music, not just the appearance of its fans and artists, that also marked punk rock as a threat. British punk rock was far more political than its American counterpart. For example, the Clash dealt with racial and economic issues in its lyrics, and the Sex Pistols lashed out against the British government and the royal family.

Unlike metal, punk rock allowed women the opportunity to participate. As Joy Press notes in her essay "Shouting Out Loud: Women in U.K. Punk," the scene was not without sexism. However, as Press explains: "In one violent swoop, punk evened the playing field for women. For the English girls who embrace it, shattering taboos and tradition was a delicious feeling." The leading women of the English punk movement included Siouxsie Sioux of Siouxsie and the Banshees, Poly Styrene of X-Ray Spex, and the bands the Slits and the Raincoats. In the United States, Patti Smith, Debbie Harry of Blondie, Tina Weymouth of the Talking Heads, and X singer

Exene Cervenka helped lead the way for women in punk.

Not surprisingly, punk also faced criticism and censorship. Much of it was directed at the Sex Pistols, whose obscenity-laden appearance on a British talk show in December 1976 sparked opprobrium throughout the English press. In addition to the print censure, the Pistols found their songs banned on radio and experienced many concert cancellations. In the United States, punk rockers were portrayed on television shows as nihilistic and violent. However, despite the danger that punk was believed to present in its early days, decades later it remains a popular genre.

The 1980s and Beyond

In August 1981, rock music changed forever with the advent of MTV. Although music videos were not new—David Bowie and other artists had been making them for more than a decade—the emergence of a cable channel devoted to videos changed the relationship between musicians and their audience. For a band to succeed, it had to combine music that connected with its audience with appealing visuals. The artists who became successful in the 1980s were not necessarily those who spoke to the concerns of the outsiders but those who made the most eye-catching videos: Duran Duran, Madonna, and Michael Jackson. With its newfound power, MTV was able to control the content of the videos it aired. Now it was not just lyrics that faced censorship but images as well; in order to have their videos broadcast, bands had to remove images that did not meet with the station's standards.

During the 1990s, "alternative" music—music that in the previous decade was generally heard only on college or independent radio stations and was largely unknown outside major markets—became one of the most popular kinds of rock music. In the early 1990s, the center of the rock universe was the Pacific Northwest. Led by Nirvana and Pearl Jam, the "Seattle sound"—also known as "grunge"—was widely popular. These bands came on the scene when rock music was dominated by pop-metal bands such as Bon Jovi and Poison. Even before the 1990s, however, Seattle had been developing its own style. In an article for the *Christian Science Monitor*, Dean Paton notes that Seattle was largely ignored by touring bands in the 1950s and 1960s because it was too far from other cities to be worth traveling to by bus. Its outsider status led the city's musicians to develop their own style. He also compares the city to Liverpool: "It is not accidental that The Beatles came from Liverpool, one of the dreariest places on earth, or that mold-breaking bands come from Seattle, one of the dreariest places in the United States." However, despite the fact that the Seattle bands of the early 1990s were all dubbed "grunge," they had very little in common sonically. For example, some of the bands turned to mid-1980s alternative bands for inspiration, while others looked to the metal or punk bands of the 1970s. The city's importance began to fade away in 1994, when Nirvana lead singer Kurt Cobain committed suicide.

Although less commercially popular than their brethren in Seattle, the cities of Olympia, Portland, and Washington, D.C., were the homes of a new type of punk rock known as "riot grrrl." These bands were composed mostly of young women with strong feminist beliefs who were dismayed by the sexism they found in much of rock. The riot grrrl scene emerged in the early 1990s and was inspired by the punk and alternative scenes in the 1970s and 1980s. Important bands included Bikini Kill, Bratmobile, and Heavens to Betsy, whose lead singer Corin Tucker would later form the influential Sleater-Kinney. For these women, riot grrrl was more than just a type of music; it was a subculture with its own values. Bands and their fans published 'zines to express their views on sexuality and politics or their struggles with sexual abuse and eating disorders. Perhaps because of its lesser popularity, the riot grrrl movement did not face the mainstream criticism of other rock subcultures.

In the late 1990s, music that combined metal with rap—a genre that had been growing increasingly popular since the 1980s—became a predominant style. Rap's popularity led to it facing many of the criticisms that rock had once garnered. Ironically, a rapper fronted one of the most controversial rock bands of the early 1990s. Ice-T and his band Body Count were widely criticized for their 1992 song "Cop Killer." After months of criticism, Warner Brothers removed the song from Body Count's album and eventually dropped the band. A more traditional rap band, 2 Live Crew, found themselves at the center of a controversy because of the lyrics of their album *As Nasty As They Wanna Be*. Criticism of rap lyrics, on the charge that the songs were too violent or misogynistic, continued through the 1990s and beyond; like rock music forty years earlier, rap concerts were often believed to encourage violence.

Although rap has received much of the negative attention since the early 1990s, rock is still seen as a threat by many conservative commentators and organizations. This became particularly clear when a number of school shootings occurred in the late 1990s. Bands such as Marilyn Manson and Rammstein were accused of influencing the actions of these teenagers through their lyrics and onstage behavior. Many bands have also been required to remove offending words or change their album covers in order to have their product sold by Walmart and other major retailers.

Changing Attitudes

Despite the continued fears, much has changed since the 1950s. Back then, many adults feared rock music. As the sales statistics from the Recording Industry Association of America indicate, that fear has changed. Between 1990 and 2000, adults aged forty-five and above doubled their share of the market and now make nearly 24 percent of music purchases. Although that share is not limited to rock music, many of these adults came of age during the rock era. Another indication that rock and roll has gained mainstream acceptance is the popularity of reunion tours staged by bands whose fan base is largely middle-aged and beyond. Finally, while the marginalized have created some of rock's most important compositions, that has not excluded musicians with college education and middle-class backgrounds from making an important creative impact. Rock music is no longer the sole purview of the outsider.

Throughout its history, rock and roll has reflected on and reacted to what was going on in society. Examining Pop Culture: *Rock and Roll* examines the origins of rock, the rise of particular genres, the controversial aspects of the music, and what the future might hold. It is hoped that the essays in this book will help readers gain a greater appreciation for rock and roll as an important and influential art form.

1

EXAMINING POP CULTURE

The Early Days of Rock and Roll

The Influence of Black Music on Rock and Roll

Charlie Gillett

In the following selection from his book, *The Sound of the City: The Rise of Rock and Roll*, Charlie Gillett details how the black musical style of rhythm and blues influenced the development of rock and roll. He explains that in the decade following World War II, rhythm and blues began to attract a white audience that was drawn to the music's beats and lyrics, with the disc jockey Alan Freed playing an important role in the music's growing popularity. White artists began to cover these songs and then write original material that both borrowed from black music and changed its character.

IN TRACING THE HISTORY OF ROCK AND ROLL, IT is useful to distinguish *rock 'n' roll*—the particular kind of music to which the term was first applied—both from *rock and roll*—the music that has been classified as such since rock 'n' roll petered out around 1958—and from *rock*, which describes post-1964 derivations of rock 'n' roll.

It is surprisingly difficult to say when rock 'n' roll "started". The term had been in use in blues songs to describe lovemaking long before it came to signify a dance beat. By 1948 it was being used in a number of songs to suggest both lovemaking and dancing—in "Good Rockin' Tonight" (recorded by Roy Brown) and in "Rock All Night Long" (the Ravens, and many

■

Excerpted from *The Sound of the City: The Rise of Rock and Roll*, by Charlie Gillett (New York: Da Capo Press, 1995). Copyright © 1970, 1995 by Charlie Gillett. Reprinted with permission.

others). In 1951 Gunter Lee Carr recorded a straight dance song, "We're Gonna Rock", dropping the sexual implication, and a year later Alan Freed, the disc jockey who was to rise to fame on rock 'n' roll, named his radio show "Moondog's Rock and Roll Party". But as a kind of music, rock 'n' roll did not make its impact on the national popular music market until 1953, when "Crazy Man Crazy", a recording by Bill Haley and His Comets, became the first rock 'n' roll song to make the best-selling lists on *Billboard*'s national chart. . . .

A Growing Market

According to a report on rhythm and blues in a special edition of *Billboard* (March 1954), the "Negro market" did not exist in a national sense until the end of the Second World War. Until that time, so-called race records, produced primarily by independent companies, tended to be distributed within particular areas—the East Coast, the Midwest, the South, the Southwest, and the West Coast. In the sixties, these areas still constituted distinct markets in that there were particular singers whose sales depended mainly on the local audiences within them. But now it is relatively easy for a company to distribute records across the country if there is a demand, which is usually created by disc jockeys playing the records in different areas.

During the ten years after the War, Los Angeles had the largest number of successful independent companies specializing in rhythm and blues. (On occasion, a few firms offered hillbilly or country and western catalogues). The companies included Specialty, Aladdin, Modern, Swingtime, and Imperial. But across the country, similar types of record companies were established from humble beginnings in garages, store-rooms, and basements, with early distribution carried out by the owners from the trunks of their cars. King, in Cincinnati; Peacock, in Houston; Chess, in Chicago; Savoy, in Newark, New Jersey; and Atlantic, in New York, were all founded between 1940 and 1950, a decade in which as many Negroes (one and a quarter million) left the South as had done so in the previous thirty years. By 1952 there were over one hundred independent companies in business (apart from many others which had failed to last), many of them specializing in rhythm and blues.

In almost every respect, the sounds of rhythm and blues

contradicted those of popular music. The vocal styles were harsh, the songs explicit, the dominant instruments—saxophone, piano, guitar, drums—were played loudly and with an emphatic dance rhythm, the production of the records was crude. The prevailing emotion was excitement.

Only some Negro records were of this type, but they were played often enough on some radio programmes to encourage the listeners who found these programmes to stay tuned. The other records played were similar to the music already familiar in the white market. But as the white listeners began to understand the different conventions by which black audiences judged their music, they came to appreciate the differences between the sing-along way white singers handled ballads, and the personal way black groups handled them.

The early and fullest impression on the new white audience of these stations was made by the dance blues—whose singers included Amos Milburn, Roy Brown, Fats Domino, and Lloyd Price—which provided a rhythm and excitement not available in white popular music. At first the number of white people interested in this music was not enough to have much effect on the sales of popular music. This portion of the audience probably consisted at first of college and a few high school students who cultivated an "R & B cult" as most of their equivalents earlier (and even then) cultivated a jazz cult.

The Minority Audience

By a happy coincidence, we happen to have some observations of remarkable insight made by the sociologist David Riesman on the popular music audience in this period, which illuminate the character of the specialist audience. In an article, "Listening to Popular Music", Riesman noted that two groups could be identified: the majority audience, which accepted the range of choices offered by the music industry and made its selections from this range without considering anything outside it; and the minority audience, which he described with details that are relevant here.

> The minority group is small. It comprises the more active listeners, who are less interested in melody or tune than in arrangement or technical virtuosity. It has developed elabo-

rate, even overelaborate, standards of music listening; hence its music listening is combined with much animated discussion of technical points and perhaps occasional reference to trade journals such as *Metronome* and *Downbeat*. The group tends to dislike name bands, most vocalists (except Negro blues singers), and radio commercials.

The rebelliousness of this minority group might be indicated in some of the following attitudes toward popular music: an insistence on rigorous standards of judgment and taste in a relativist culture; a preference for the uncommercialized, unadvertised small bands rather than name bands; the development of a private language and then a flight from it when the private language (the same is true of other aspects of private style) is taken over by the majority group; a profound resentment of the commercialization of radio and musicians. Dissident attitudes toward competition and cooperation in our culture might be represented in feelings about improvisation and small "combos"; an appreciation for idiosyncrasy of performance goes together with a dislike of "star" performers and an insistence that the improvisation be a group-generated phenomenon.

There are still other ways in which the minority may use popular music to polarize itself from the majority group, and thereby from American popular culture generally: a sympathetic attitude or even preference for Negro musicians; an egalitarian attitude toward the roles, in love and work, of the two sexes; a more international outlook, with or without awareness, for example, of French interest in American jazz; an identification with disadvantaged groups, not only Negroes, from which jazz springs, with or without a romantic cult of proletarianism; a dislike of romantic pseudo-sexuality in music, even without any articulate awareness of being exploited; similarly a reaction against the stylized body image and limitations of physical self-expression which "sweet" music and its lyrics are felt as conveying; a feeling that music is too important to serve as a backdrop for dancing, small talk, studying, and the like; a diffuse resentment of the image of the teen-ager provided by the mass media.

To carry matters beyond this descriptive suggestion of majority and minority patterns requires an analysis of the social structure in which the teen-ager finds himself. When he listens to music, even if no one else is around, he listens in a context of imaginary "others"—his listening is indeed often an effort to establish connection with them. In general what he perceives in the mass media is framed by his perception of the peer-groups to which he belongs. These groups not only rate the tunes but select for their members in more subtle ways what is to be "heard" in each tune. It is the pressure of conformity with the group that invites and compels the individual to have recourse to the media both in order to learn from them what the group expects and to identify with the group by sharing a common focus for attention and talk.

Riesman's observation that no matter what the majority chooses, there will be a minority choosing something different explains how popular music continues to change, no matter how good—or bad—the dominant types of music are at any particular period. And because the minority audience defines itself as being radical within the music audience, its taste is likely to favour, consciously or unconsciously, music with some element of social comment or criticism in it.

Alan Freed's Role

During the early fifties, young people like those described by Riesman turned in increasing numbers to rhythm and blues music, and to the radio stations that broadcast it. If the first listeners were those with relatively sophisticated standards for judging music, those that came later included many whose taste was more instinctive, who liked the dance beat or the thrilling effect of a hard-blown saxophone, people who may have found the rough voices of the singers a bit quaint and appealing as novelties.

It was this second group of listeners who provided the inspiration and audience for Alan Freed, who, with Bill Haley, played a crucial role in popularizing rhythm and blues under the name "rock 'n' roll".

Alan Freed was a disc jockey on an evening classical music programme in Cleveland, Ohio, when he was invited, sometime in 1952, to visit a downtown record store by the owner,

Leo Mintz. Mintz was intrigued by the musical taste of some of the white adolescents who bought records at his store, and Freed was amazed by it. He watched the excited reaction of the youths who danced energetically as they listened to music that Freed had previously considered alien to their culture—rhythm and blues. He recalled (in the British *New Musical Express*, September 23, 1956):

> I heard the tenor saxophones of Red Prysock and Big Al Sears. I heard the blues-singing, piano-playing Ivory Joe Hunter. I wondered. I wondered for about a week. Then I went to the station manager and talked him into permitting me to follow my classical programme with a rock 'n' roll party.

At Mintz's suggestion, Freed introduced a euphemism for rhythm and blues by calling his show "Moondog's Rock 'n' Roll Party", which started in June 1951. By March 1952, Freed was convinced he had enough listeners to justify promoting a concert featuring some of the artists whose records he had been playing. "Moondog's Coronation Ball" was to be staged at the Cleveland Arena, capacity 10,000; but according to firemen's estimates more than 21,000 people showed up, mostly black, causing such a panic that the show had to be called off (as reported in the *Cleveland Press*). Abandoning the idea of holding mammoth dances, Freed persevered with reserved-seat shows, and climaxed his career in Cleveland, in August 1953, with a bill that featured the Buddy Johnson Orchestra, Joe Turner, Fats Domino, the Moonglows, the Harptones, the Drifters, Ella Johnson, Dakota Staton, and Red Prysock.

Freed's success among white audiences with Negro music was widely reported in *Billboard*, and in 1954 he was signed by a New York station, WINS, which he quickly established as New York's leading popular music station. He continued to champion the original Negro performers of songs which were "covered"—recorded by someone else—for the white market by the major companies, and in interviews he accused other disc jockeys of prejudice when they preferred to play the cover versions.

Once the new audience became apparent, juke-box distributors began putting rock 'n' roll records in juke boxes, which then provided a new channel of communication for white record buyers who did not yet tune in to the Negro radio stations. At the same time, in response to the new demand for uptempo dance tunes with a black beat from audiences at dance halls, a number of white groups were incorporating rhythm-and-blues-type material into the repertoires. It was with such a song, "Crazy Man Crazy", recorded for the independent Essex, that Bill Haley and His Comets made their first hit parade appearance in 1953 and pushed rock 'n' roll up another rung of popular attention.

Bill Haley Changes Music

By the end of 1953, at which point the Negro market comprised only 5.7 per cent of the total American record sales market, a number of people in the music industry were beginning to realize the potential of Negro music and styles for at least a segment of the white market. Decca took a chance and considerably outpaced its rival major companies by contracting Haley from Essex. At his first session with Decca, he recorded "Rock Around the Clock" and "Shake, Rattle and Roll", which between them were to transform throughout the world the conception of what popular music could be.

Haley's records were not straight copies of any particular black style or record. The singer's voice was unmistakably white, and the repetitive choral chants were a familiar part of many "swing" bands. In these respects the music was similar to a style known as "western swing" (and in particular a group called Bob Wills and His Texas Playboys). But the novel feature of Haley's style, its rhythm, was drawn from black music, although in Haley the rhythm dominated the arrangements much more than it did in Negro records. With Haley, every other beat was heavily accented by the singers and all the instrumentalists at the expense of the relatively flexible rhythms and complex harmonies of dance music records cut for the black audience.

"Shake, Rattle and Roll" was in the top ten for twelve weeks from September 1954; "Rock Around the Clock" was in the list for nineteen weeks, including eight at the top, from May 1955. By the summer of 1955, roughly two years after Haley's "Crazy Man Crazy", with most of the majors still moving uncertainly, the demand for records with an insistent dance beat was sufficient for three independently manufactured records to reach the top ten in record sales—"Seventeen" by Boyd Bennett (King), "Ain't That a Shame" by Pat Boone (Dot), and "Maybellene" by Chuck Berry (Chess), the last recorded by a black singer. . . .

A Change in the Music

Although Alan Freed did not, as he sometimes claimed, coin the expression "rock 'n' roll" or create a new music single-handed, he did play an incalculable role in developing the concept of an exciting music that could express the feelings of adolescence. When he first used the term "rock 'n' roll", he was applying it to music that already existed under another name, "rhythm and blues". But the change in name induced a change in the music itself. "Rhythm and blues" had meant music by black people for black people. "Rock 'n' roll" meant at first only that this music was being directed at white listeners, but then, as the people producing the music became conscious of their new audience, they changed the character of the music, so that "rock 'n' roll" came to describe—and be—something different from "rhythm and blues".

How the South Shaped Elvis Presley

John Shelton Reed

John Shelton Reed explains how Elvis Presley's childhood in Tupelo, Mississippi, shaped the singer and his music. Reed maintains that Presley had an exceptionally ordinary upbringing and that his parents worked in the jobs typical of 1930s Tupelo. Although Tupelo was better off than much of the rest of Mississippi, it had its share of economic troubles. Reed explains that Elvis spent his childhood in a city that was centered around religion and segregation, but that when he burst onto the music scene as a nineteen-year-old, he did so by covering a rhythm-and-blues song, thus symbolizing the end of segregation in the South. Reed is a professor emeritus of sociology at the University of North Carolina at Chapel Hill and the former director of the Institute for Research in Social Science.

ELVIS HAD AN EXTRAORDINARY TALENT, BUT HE also had the great good fortune to be in the right place at the right time for that talent to be recognized and acclaimed. His flower didn't bloom unseen or waste its sweetness very long on the desert air of the First Assembly of God. But whatever the balance of individual genius and social readiness to nurture and to reward it, the combination has clearly made him a figure of unique cultural importance.

∎

So I thought I'd begin with how Elvis was *not* unique—how he was, in many ways, quite ordinary. In most respects, it would interest a sociologist that he was born and raised in an ordinary southern white family, and that he was born and raised in an ordinary southern town. You could even say that the Presleys and Tupelo were extraordinarily ordinary—not just typical but exemplary. The histories of the Presleys and of Tupelo illustrate much broader themes in southern history; one way or another they illustrate important trends from the collapse of cotton tenancy to the rise of Pentecostalism, and implicate high-profile southern institutions from Parchman penitentiary to TVA.

It's worth emphasizing Elvis's ordinariness, I think, because that's part of his fascination and his appeal. Although he became a remarkable cultural phenomenon, his background and first nineteen years were, in broad outline, much the same as those of hundreds of thousands of other southern white boys. To understand how he was unique, we have to start by understanding how he wasn't. To understand him, you have to understand where he came from. You can't *stop* there, but that's where you have to start.

Elvis's Parents

He was born, of course, in 1935, in Tupelo, the son of Vernon Presley and the former Gladys Smith, and, as Elaine Dundy's genealogical research makes clear, even his ancestry was typical for a southern white boy. Elvis's ancestors, like those of most white southerners, were mostly British. The Smiths, his mother's family, were of English descent, moving west from South Carolina after the Civil War, but most of the rest were Celtic rather than Anglo-Saxon. The Presley name came to America with Scots who settled in North Carolina in the eighteenth century, then moved south and west over the years. Most of Elvis's other ancestors were Scotch-*Irish*, part of the great wave of migration from Scotland to Ulster to Pennsylvania, then down the Shenandoah Valley to the southern interior from southwest Virginia to Texas. . . .

When Vernon Presley and Gladys Smith moved to East Tupelo, they were among the first of their families to leave the land: Gladys to run a sewing machine in the Tupelo Garment

Center for $2 a day; Vernon to pursue a string of odd but definitely urban jobs—milkman, cabinetmaker, lumberyard worker, delivery-truck driver (delivering wholesale groceries and also, it appears, bootleg liquor).

Incidentally, Gladys was not unusual in being a working woman. In this century, southern women have actually been more likely than women elsewhere to work outside their homes. Many of them—and probably most of their men—would have preferred it otherwise, but economic circumstances made it necessary. This was certainly true for the Presleys. Whenever the family could afford it, Gladys left the labor force. But they could seldom afford it. She worked for the garment factory before and during her pregnancy. She picked cotton with the young Elvis sitting on her picking sack. She worked at the Mid-South Laundry. After the family moved to Memphis she found work immediately as a seamstress for Fashion Curtains. Later she worked in a cafeteria, then as a nurse's aide.

In moving to Tupelo the Presleys were a small part of a great demographic trend that moved rural southerners into towns, farmers into industrial and service occupations. Vernon and Gladys were only a generation ahead of the Hale County, Alabama, families that were portrayed by James Agee and Walker Evans in *Let Us Now Praise Famous Men*. Those families were still sharecropping when Agee and Evans paid their famous visit in the late 1930s; forty years later their children had made the same transition Vernon and Gladys made: Both men and women were working in service and industrial occupations—welder, meatpacker, nursing-home attendant, and so forth. Economically, they were still near the bottom, but the bottom wasn't nearly so low as it had been in the 1930s.

The Economy of 1930s South

When Elvis was born, two-thirds of all southerners lived in the countryside and half the South's labor force were farmers; by the time of his death, two-thirds of southerners were urban and suburban folk; fewer than 5 percent were farmers and the sharecropper was an endangered species.

What kind of place was Tupelo when the young Presley family lived there? It was very different from the town of today. And it was part of a state and a region that were very different from what *they* are today. An Englishman named L. P. Hartley once wrote, "The past is a foreign country; they do things differently there"—and certainly that's true for the American South. In my experience as a teacher, I've found it almost impossible for young people today really to understand what it meant to live in the South of the 1930s. What it meant to live with the day-to-day constraints and indignities of Jim Crow—not just to live with them, but to take them for granted as simply *how things are*. What it meant to live in a region as poor as the South—a region with a per capita income about the same as that of Venezuela's today, about half of what it was elsewhere in the United States. We need to recognize that those among us who once lived in that South—those who, like the Presleys, grew up in that "foreign country" of the past— made a transition in their lifetimes as dramatic and sometimes as wrenching as emigration.

In 1938 Franklin Roosevelt would describe the entire South as "the Nation's No. 1 economic problem"—this with the Depression going on. A government commission had drawn a picture of poverty, dependence, ignorance, disease, malnutrition, inadequate housing, and environmental degradation that closely parallels accounts of life in the Third World today. The researches of Howard Odum and his colleagues at North Carolina, Charles Johnson at Fisk, and other sociologists of the 1930s provided the basis for that report and showed that the South's problems were concentrated in the old Cotton Belt of the Deep South, that long arc from eastern North Carolina to east Texas where the shadow of the plantation still lingered. In this respect, as in many others, Mississippi was the most southern of the southern states. In 1931 H.L. Mencken had put together indicators of health, literacy, economic well-being, and so forth to show readers of the *American Mercury* that what he called "the level of civilization" was lower in the former Confederate states than anywhere else in the country. And by these measures, Mencken announced, "the worst American state" was Mississippi.

In the year of Elvis's birth, Tupelo was home to some 7,000 souls and served another 30,000 residents of Lee County as a market, banking, and shopping center. Two-thirds of the county's residents were white; only a couple dozen were foreign-born. Outside Tupelo, four out of five Lee Countians lived on farms, most of them growing cotton, many—like Elvis's grandparents—as tenants or sharecroppers. Vaughan Grisham calculates that in 1930 the cash income of the average Lee County cotton farmer had fallen to something on the order of $200, *before* paying loan interest, fertilizer bills, and the like. Tupelo was in many respects a typical Cotton Belt county seat, and to the considerable extent that its prosperity was tied up with the cotton economy, the town was in serious trouble—like the South as a whole. But in some ways the town was unusual, certainly for Mississippi. It had hedged its economic bets, and it pointed the way to the South's future. . . .

African American Influences on Elvis

Elvis didn't always appear fully white. Not sounding white was his first problem, and white radio stations were initially reluctant to play his records. Not to be clearly white was dangerous because it undermined the black-white rigidities of a segregated society, and to blur those definitions was to reveal the falseness at the core of segregation. Racial ambiguity is both the internal moral condemnation and the social destruction of a racist society which can only pretend to justify itself by abiding by its own taboos. Yet all Southerners know, despite the sternest Jim Crow laws, that more than two hundred years of racial mixing has left many a Southerner racially ambiguous. White Southerners admit only the reality of blacks who have some white blood, but, of course, the knife cuts both ways. . . . In most pictures, Elvis might resemble a blue-eyed Adonis, but in some of those early black and white photographs, his eyes sultry, nostrils flared, lips sullen, he looked just that—black and white. And he dressed like blacks. His early wardrobe came from Lansky Brothers in Memphis. Maybe truck drivers wore greasy hair and long sideburns, but only

Race and Religion

[One] aspect of Tupelo that its boosters didn't emphasize was its pattern of race relations. Day-to-day, the races rubbed along together, but they did it within the usual southern framework of black disenfranchisement, segregation of public facilities and much of private life, petty harassment, and occasionally brutal intimidation. Grisham recounts, for example, the routine humiliations black Tupeloans experienced at the hands of the police. Many responded by joining the Great Migration that took millions of southern blacks from the rural and small-town South to southern cities and beyond, to the cities of the Northeast and Midwest.

the blacks were wearing zoot suits and pegged pants with pink darts in them. Country singers might sequin cactus and saddles on satin shirts, Marty Robbins would put a pink carnation on a white sport coat, and Johnny Cash would be the man in black. Only Elvis would wear a pink sport coat with a black velvet collar. "The Memphis Flash," he was sometimes called.

The music was the obvious racial ambiguity. Elvis' use of black styles and black music angered many Southern blacks who resented the success he won with music that black artists had originated but could not sell beyond the "race record" market of a segregated commercial world. In interviews today, these black blues musicians usually say that Elvis stole everything from them, an understandable complaint but one that nevertheless ignores his fusion of black music with white country to create a genuinely new sound. He was the Hillbilly Cat singing "Blue Moon of Kentucky" and "That's All Right (Mama)." Elvis' role in fusing the native music of poor Southern whites and poor Southern blacks into rock and roll is the best known aspect of his career and his greatest accomplishment.

Linda Ray Pratt, "Elvis, or the Ironies of Southern Identity," in *Rock Music in America*, ed. Janet Podell, 1987.

Congressman [John Elliott] Rankin may have been a great champion of the Tennessee Valley Authority (TVA), but he was better known throughout the nation as a race-baiting southern demagogue. His political career began after World War I when he founded a racist newspaper called *New Era*. Grisham summarizes what that paper was all about: "The favorite themes were the defense of lynchings, pleas for the repudiation of the Fifteenth Amendment and alterations of the Fourteenth Amendment of the Constitution, and general assaults on 'do-good troublemakers.'" Rankin used this platform to get elected to Congress in 1920. A black leader commented later, "Thank God Mr. Rankin got himself sent to Washington or I suppose all of us colored people would have had to leave Tupelo." When Elvis was ten years old his congressman was still running against "interests outside the state who literally hate the white people of the South and want to destroy everything for which we stand."

But it tells us something about Tupelo that Rankin was finally unseated in 1952, when his rhetoric came to be seen as an impediment to industrialization. Although being black in Tupelo was no picnic, the town's boosterism spared it the worst excesses of Jim Crow's death throes. Grisham tells a revealing story. He spoke to a segregationist who had sworn to kill anyone advocating desegregation, and asked him about the editor of the *Tupelo Daily Journal*, who had been a moderate, even liberal, voice in race relations. The man replied, "I just knew that George McLean [the editor] was a God-damned Communist, but he was the man who was bringing jobs into the area and if anything happened to him we would have all been sunk." All in all, it seems Tupelo was something of a vest-pocket, Mississippi version of Atlanta, "the city too busy to hate."

So much for the town's economic and political institutions, and they are certainly much of what made Tupelo Tupelo. But there were other institutions that were equally important in shaping the life of the town. Although the WPA guide didn't mention it, Tupelo, like almost every other southern town, was a city of churches—dozens of them in the town and the nearby countryside, ranging from the big Baptist and Methodist establishments downtown to the more modest churches and tabernacles serving the white mill workers and common folk of East and South Tupelo and the black residents of Tupelo's three Negro sections. Two Tupelo churches figure prominently in Elvis's story.

One, of course, is the Assembly of God in East Tupelo, the church the Presleys attended. It was built by the Reverend Gains Mansell, Gladys's uncle, and after World War II Vernon himself became a deacon. The denomination was a new one—founded in Hot Springs, Arkansas, in 1914, it was a mere twenty years old when Elvis was born—but it was one of the fastest-growing of the great family of Pentecostal and Holiness groups that trace their origins to what some have called the "Third Great Awakening" at the turn of the century. Some of those groups are black, some are white, a few are strikingly both, but all believe in such gifts of the Holy Spirit as speaking in tongues; most practice faith healing, foot washing, and other activities found in scripture; nearly all have traditions of lively and powerful gospel music; and none gets much respect from uptown Christians, much less from secular humanists.

The other Tupelo church that figures in our story is the Sanctified Church, which met in a permanent tent in the black neighborhood of Shake Rag. After the Presley's moved from East Tupelo into town they lived on the edge of Shake Rag, and much speculation has centered on how much exposure the young Elvis had to the black gospel music being performed down the street from his house. After he moved to Memphis, of course, we don't have to speculate.

So this was the town in which Elvis was born and in which he spent his first thirteen years. . . .

Musical and Political Integration

When the Presleys left Tupelo for the big city, once again they were a typical part of a larger picture. Vaughan Grisham reports that 20 percent of Mississippi's population left the state during the 1950s, the culmination of a movement from the rural and small-town South that was one of the great mass migrations of human history. In 1960, 10 million Americans born in the South were living outside the region altogether, mostly in northern cities. We hear a lot about the Great Migration of blacks, but two-thirds of that 10 million were white.

On May 17, 1954, the Supreme Court handed down its

historic decision in *Brown v. Board of Education*, a day that came to be known in some white southern circles as "Black Monday." It marked the beginning of the end of Jim Crow, of de jure racial segregation in the South. Seven weeks later to the day, on another Monday, July 5, Elvis recorded a country-flavored version of the rhythm-and-blues hit "That's All Right, Mama," an act of *musical* integration that set the stage for rock and roll. And he knew what he was doing. He said, "The colored folks been singing it and playing it just like I'm doin' now, man, for more years than I know. They played it like that in the shanties and in their juke joints, and nobody paid it no mind 'til I goosed it up." That spring of 1954 Elvis, like the South as a whole, took a big step into the unknown, and neither would ever be the same.

The Spread of Rock Music in England

Peter Wicke

The music scene in 1950s Great Britain was largely conservative, shaped by the strictures of the British Broadcast Corporation. In the following selection, Peter Wicke details how the entrance of rock music during that decade had a tremendous cultural impact on British youth, in particular working-class teenagers. He suggests that rock music gave these teenagers a way to develop their own lifestyle and culture, one that stood in sharp contrast to the era's conservative political establishment. Wicke is the director of the Centre for Popular Music Research in the Music Programology at Berlin's Humboldt University.

IN THE FIFTIES THE BRITISH BROADCASTING Corporation (BBC), in its role as the British national cultural institution, . . . possessed almost unlimited authority in all questions of the nation's musical entertainment. The only alternatives to the BBC were the English evening programmes of Radio Luxembourg and the commercial television station Independent Television (ITV), finally approved by the British Government in 1954 after long discussions. At that time ITV hardly affected the development of pop music. Radio Luxembourg on the other hand, a radio station modelled on American radio, reached a not inconsiderable audience of young people in England but was situated on the Continent and was

■

therefore only of limited interest to the British music industry. The authority whose programming policies exercised by far the greatest influence both on the nation's musical taste and on the British music industry was the BBC. But the BBC was dominated by an unparalleled conservatism which felt the new teenage musical needs emerging in the fifties were linked to the nightmare of the decline of culture and education in a commercial mass culture modelled on the American experience. . . .

A Conservative Approach to Music

The large record companies, foremost among them EMI, naturally adjusted to the guidelines of BBC programming policy and only concentrated on those releases which, in view of the existing limitations of the needle-time agreement, had any chance of being considered for the broadcasting playlist, one of the main tools of sales promotion. Hunter Davies, the first biographer of the Beatles, described this quite clearly:

> It was like bringing out a regular monthly magazine. Each month a company like Parlophone brought out around ten new records, all planned about two months ahead, which they called their monthly supplements. They were always very strictly and fairly balanced. Out of the ten new records two would be classical, two jazz, two dance music—the Victor Sylvester sort of dance music—two would be male vocal and two would be female vocal.

Like everything else this too was conservative, firmly rooted in habits whose only justification was that things had always been done that way.

Bill Haley's 'Rock Around the Clock', released in Britain in 1954 on the Decca Brunswick label, really exploded onto this soft British musical entertainment scene. The contrast could not have been greater. It was also the first single to sell more than a million copies in Britain. This was the signal for a radically different style of leisure behaviour, particularly among British working-class teenagers, for as the sociologists and consumer strategists quickly found out:

> the teenage market is almost entirely working class. Its middle class members are either still at school and college or

else just beginning on their careers: in either case they dispose of much smaller incomes than their working class contemporaries and it is highly probable, therefore, that not far short of 90 per cent of all teenage spending is conditioned by working class taste and values.

Rock'n'roll made it obvious for the first time in Britain that working-class teenagers were beginning to form cultural value patterns in their leisure which were increasingly clearly contrasted with the official cultural institutions. Just the fact that 'Rock Around the Clock' was an American production shocked the officials of British culture. . . .

Rock Becomes a Cultural Force

Rock'n'roll promoted the utopia of a distant America, a utopia which could encompass the everyday experiences of British working-class teenagers with all their longings, desires, hopes, frustrations and leisure needs. Rock'n'roll mediated a self-image to these teenagers, which—influenced by the values and leisure patterns of American high school students—was literally miles away from their actual situation, but which despite this could only find its basis in the structure of their daily lives. It took the experience of daily life in the dismal English working-class suburbs, where the cinema was the only remaining alternative to the street, to see rock'n'roll as an opportunity for cultural realisation, an opportunity which was able to break down the constricting boundaries of school, work and the family home by making them able to feel an undefined longing for something 'real' which had to exist somewhere beyond the oppressive ordinariness of life. Thus, with a provocative challenge rock'n'roll bore witness to the social and cultural claims of British working-class teenagers, even though these claims were expressed via a foreign identity. Dick Hebdige's expression, a 'stolen form', neatly picks up this point.

Against this background, rock'n'roll achieved a significance in Britain which it had never possessed in America. In fifties Britain it became the cultural symbol of working-class teenagers. To conservative public opinion as expressed in the media, this situation logically represented an external attack on the supposed 'classlessness', an attack which considerably disturbed the 'social peace' of the nation. When the rise of

British beat music made the argument that British culture was being swamped by American music imports untenable, reactions sharpened, thereby reinforcing the link between this music and the social problems of the working-class teenager. Music became a convenient symbol in the increasingly sharp conflict. The fact that teenagers themselves took this conflict quite personally—equating it with clashes with their parents, with school, with the world around them, with the problems of getting a job, with their superiors at work—did not change the social nature of the conflict at all. This was not the private conflict of a restless youth, the so-called 'generation conflict', but was rather concerned with the opportunities for developing a lifestyle and culture suited to the class-specific experience of the changing face of British capitalism. It is not surprising that ruling conservative opinion considered this a threat. The *New Statesman*, the opinion leader of the political establishment, in 1964 described the 'menace of Beatleism':

> Both T.V. channels now run weekly programmes in which popular records are played to teenagers and judged. While the music is performed, the cameras linger savagely over the faces of the audience. What a bottomless chasm of vacuity they reveal. Huge faces, bloated with cheap confectionery and smeared with chain-store make-up, the open, sagging mouths and glazed eyes, the hands mindlessly drumming in time to the music, the broken stiletto heels, the shoddy, stereotyped, 'with-it' clothes: here, apparently, is a collective portrait of a generation enslaved by a commercial machine.

Such distorted images dominated public discussion about British beat music and also formed the background which gave a song like the Beatles' 'Love Me Do' its explosive force. The contradiction that it was precisely the political apologists of a commerce-led consumer society who were complaining about the reality of such commerce is only an apparent one. Just as the powerful control centres of monopoly capital had a basic interest in maintaining the ideology of the 'classless consumer society', so the music industry, once it had discovered the commercial potential of the beat boom, had an equally direct interest in its exploitation, whether this suited the official model of a uniform consumer culture or not. The arguments were not about a socially meaningful development of mass culture, but were between two factions of the ruling power structure— the political representatives of state authority in the interests of monopoly capital and the financial empires of the culture and music industry—over control of any such development.

It was this background which gave rock'n'roll in Britain and British beat music its spectacular significance, and which allowed music to become the symbol of a deep cultural conflict. This conflict brought with it a polarisation between the class-specific cultural claims of working-class youth and the cultural representation of a supposedly classless consumer society. Within this conflict rock'n'roll, as played by young amateur groups, was transformed by an aesthetic which caused far-reaching changes in popular music. The amateur bands chose to play those rock'n'roll songs which meant something to them and their audience. However, their choice was definitely influenced in part by the context in which this music found itself in Britain. The mere fact that there was such a broad amateur music movement looking for its roots in a music form imported from abroad cannot have been pure chance. . . .

Finding Meaning in the Music

Of course, the fact that British working-class teenagers in particular identified with rock'n'roll and, in playing it, developed a musical form which more directly suited their needs and the structures of meaning of their leisure, was not due to any arbitrary act nor to pure chance. In the first place this naturally had something to do with the musical qualities of rock'n'roll, and secondly it was linked to the particular musical nature of individual songs, for these songs were not played indiscriminately. Mike Howes, a producer with his own studio complex in Liverpool, was one of the working-class youngsters who crowded the beat clubs night after night, and reported: 'At that time it was black rock'n'roll that particularly appealed to us, the songs of Chuck Berry, Little Richard and Fats Domino. The bands who could play these songs best were the most popular, and the Beatles were among them. This was around 1960/61.'

What was important was rock'n'roll's dance music qualities and the songs from the Afro-American tradition were the ones which suited this best. The songs which exercised the greatest influence on early British beat music were those with the most motoric energy, like Chuck Berry's 'Roll Over Beethoven'. It was not by chance that this song was in the Beatles' repertoire together with a number of other Berry songs. Dancing itself was, of course, already a central element of teenage leisure activity and, together with music, created their own leisure environment. But at the same time it was the form of the literal appropriation of the rock'n'roll songs which made them open to *their* meanings and open to being *their* medium of expression. In sensuous identification with the music through bodily movement in dance, the structures of the songs were dissolved into patterns and images of movement. It was not their meaning, their content, that was 'read' but their movement; they were not merely heard but rather physically deciphered. And it was exactly this which formed the basis for the construction of a second, symbolic, system of meaning over the immediate content, a system of meaning which, without being obvious in the songs and without being fixed in meaning by the lyrics and music, is nevertheless not independent of them. Teenagers stripped rock'n'roll songs of their concrete determinacy of meaning by changing them into patterns of movement while they were dancing. And as patterns of movement they could be assimilated into the structures of their lifestyle and leisure and could then themselves function as the material of a more comprehensive system of meaning, combined with other material such as clothes, hairstyles, gestures (coolness, etc.) and styles of speech (slang) as elements in a complex cultural style of behaviour. But for this to happen, the utopia of a distant America, mediated through the lyrics, was anything but unimportant.

The Beatles and the Creation of a New British Sound

David Hatch and Stephen Millward

The Beatles are widely considered to be the most influential group in the history of rock. In the following excerpt from their book *From Blues to Rock: An Analytical History of Pop Music*, David Hatch and Stephen Millward explain how the Liverpool band created a new type of British music that stood apart from its American predecessors. According to the authors, the Beatles were influenced first by 1950s stars such as Elvis Presley and Chuck Berry and then by contemporary rhythm and blues. However, by 1965 the Beatles had ceased covering songs and were instead recording original music that emphasized their unique vocal and instrumental style. Their new approach inspired their peers and led to a changing relationship between American and British music.

JOHN LENNON WAS INFATUATED WITH ROCK & roll as a teenager. He became particularly obsessed by Elvis Presley: his Aunt Mimi recalled, in an interview quoted by Philip Norman, 'I never got a minute's peace. It was Elvis Presley, Elvis Presley, Elvis Presley. In the end I said, "Elvis Presley's all very well, John, but I don't want him for breakfast, dinner *and* tea."' His interest in the music never really left him. His first studio album after the demise of the Beatles, *John Lennon/Plastic Ono Band*, included three items with a heavy

■

back-beat ('Remember', 'Well, Well Well', and 'I Found Out') and featured throughout pronounced echo on the vocal track, a device which was to become a distinctive characteristic of his solo work. In 1975, Lennon released *Rock 'N' Roll* which consisted in the main of the 1950s material of such artists as Chuck Berry, Little Richard, and Fats Domino.

Paul McCartney was accepted as a member of the Quarry Men (the earliest incarnation of the Beatles) only because he knew the chords to Eddie Cochran's 'Twenty Flight Rock'. Although his music no longer bears any resemblance to rock & roll, his affection for the music is still apparent. On the BBC Radio Programme 'Desert Island Discs', broadcast in the early 1980s, McCartney chose five rock & roll records in his allocation of eight selections.

Early Influences on the Beatles

It is not surprising, therefore, to learn that the Beatles concentrated on rock & roll material during their residencies in Hamburg, which commenced in the summer of 1960. Included in their repertoire were such items as Carl Perkins's 'Honey Don't' and Chuck Berry's 'Too Much Monkey Business' as well as latter day Presley hits such as 'Love Me Tender'. Yet at their first recording sessions for Parlophone, in September 1962 and February 1963, which yielded their first two hit singles and the whole of their first album *(Please Please Me)*, the emphasis was upon contemporary rhythm & blues and the compositions of Lennon and McCartney. This formula was repeated for their second album, *With The Beatles*. In fact, the only incontestably rock & roll song appeared on that second LP release, namely Chuck Berry's 'Roll Over Beethoven'.

It could be argued that by that stage the rock & roll of the 1950s was no longer a commercial proposition, and that the Beatles chose instead to turn their attention to what might be regarded as 'underground' music as yet unfamiliar to most British record-buyers. However, the Beatles' apprenticeship in rock & roll informed their work on the early albums in certain crucial respects.

Most notably, the singing of McCartney and, in particular, Lennon, brought a rock & roll character to both their own originals and the R. & B. material they took on. Lennon, for example, did not attempt to copy the vocal styles of Smokey Robinson and Barrett Strong in the versions of, respectively, 'You Really Gotta Hold On Me' and 'Money'. His own methods were already developed by then, namely the rasping delivery and uninhibited approach of his mentors. In this way, Lennon and McCartney were free to handle what was largely obscure material in any case in an essentially personal fashion.

The Beatles Popularized New Ideas

[The Beatles] were never pure forerunners. The Yardbirds used the sitar before the Beatles: the Beach Boys were experimenting with studio enhancement first; the Four Seasons were using elaborate harmonies before the Beatles. They were never as contemptuously anti-middle-class or decadent as the Kinks or the Rolling Stones; never as lyrically compelling as Dylan; never as musically brilliant as the Band; never as hallucinogenic as the San Francisco groups. John Gabree, one of the most perceptive of the early rock writers, said that "their job, and they have done it well, has been to travel a few miles behind the avant-garde, consolidating gains and popularizing new ideas."

Yet this very willingness meant that new ideas did not struggle and die in obscurity; instead, they touched a hundred million minds. Their songs reflected the widest range of mood of any group of their time. Their openness created a kind of salon for a whole generation of people, an idea exchange into which the youth of the world was wired. It was almost inevitable that, even against their will, their listeners shaped a dream of politics and life-style from the substance of popular music. It is testament both to the power of rock music, and to the illusions which can be spun out of impulses.

Jeff Greenfield, *New York Times Magazine*, February 16, 1975.

This process was complemented by the fact that the Beatles tended to slow down the tempos of the original recordings for greater effect, examples of which include their treatment of Arthur Alexander's 'Anna' and the Shirelles' 'Baby It's You'.

Similarly, their instrumental work, while perhaps lacking the fluency and timing of the American product, compensates by supplying an attack and intensity clearly derived from prolonged exposure to rock & roll. In this respect, their version of 'Money' can almost be said to prefigure the 'heavy rock' methods of several years later.

Creating a Distinctive Sound

The result of such processes was a music which sounded distinctive *and* authentic. On hearing 'Love Me Do' for the first time, many listeners assumed that it was the work of a black group or, at the very least, that it was American in origin. Of course Lennon and McCartney also discovered that they had the ability to compose commercially successful pop tunes, a fact which has tended to obscure their efforts in other directions. Their involvement with rock & roll cannot be said to have influenced these songs, with the possible exception of such early efforts as 'I Saw Her Standing There'. While it is true that an R. & B. influence is apparent in certain originals, for example, 'All I've Got To Do', 'Little Child', and 'Not A Second Time', these compositions can hardly be counted as being among their most popular. Yet at least the overtly commercial material the Beatles produced *was* their own: antipathy to Tin Pan Alley is illustrated by the fact that they withstood pressure to record 'How Do You Do It' (composed by the professional writer Mitch Murray) at their first session. The song was subsequently a number one hit in Britain for Gerry and the Pacemakers.

Rock & roll songs such as 'Long Tall Sally' and 'Honey Don't' continued to appear occasionally on Beatles releases and in their stage-act, culminating in their version of Larry Williams's 'Dizzy Miss Lizzy' on the *Help!* album of 1965. This, and 'Act Naturally' from the same LP, were to be the last items not to be composed by members of the band until the 39-second fragment of the Liverpool folk-song, 'Maggie Mae', appeared on the Beatles' final album release *Let It Be*.

In December 1965, they issued the LP *Rubber Soul*, and the transition to wholly original material was completed. This now bore little relation to their early recordings. The songs were more personal in content, making use of lyrical conceits and instrumental arrangements, the nature of which was entirely individual. (George Harrison was reportedly outraged at the Hollies' cover version of his 'If I Needed Someone'.) The subject matter of many of the compositions was certainly striking and completely foreign to the British pop music of the period, especially in the songs on which Lennon seemed to be the dominant influence, for example 'Nowhere Man', 'Norwegian Wood', and 'In My Life'. Furthermore, the Beatles were beginning to discover the possibilities opened up by four-track recording—principally the way in which sound could be 'layered' over a period of time to create something aurally distinctive.

Links with American rhythm & blues and rock & roll were now severed. The Beatles had established a tradition of British pop music, a development totally without precedent. Other artists, most notably The Who, now concerned themselves with reflecting their own environment, rather than borrowing images and inspiration from elsewhere. It should be reiterated, however, that this state of affairs was not created in a vacuum. The Beatles' assimilation of rock & roll into their music was crucial in providing for the conditions under which further development could take place. Additionally, their work heralded a new competence among British musicians, a vital factor in the formation of rock. The relationship between American and British music was destined to continue, resulting in further important changes during the mid-1960s.

EXAMINING POP CULTURE

The Politics
of Rock

Protest Music in the 1960s

Jerome L. Rodnitzky

Folk music has been an important current in American pop culture since the 1930s. The genre experienced a renaissance in the 1960s, at a time when songwriters began to focus on issues such as the Vietnam War, civil rights, the environment, and feminism. In the following selection, Jerome L. Rodnitzky provides an overview of 1960s protest music. At first, these songs dealt with specific and topical issues. Key artists included Pete Seeger, who consistently championed social causes in his folk music. However, folk music began to change in the mid-1960s. Bob Dylan's decision to move from the acoustic to the electric guitar led to the development of folk-rock. In addition to the different instrumentation, the lyrical content of the music changed. Instead of tackling specific topics, songwriters began to express vaguer expressions of discontent. By 1966, protest music had lost much of its power. Songs continued to be written about the war and dangers to the environment, but those songs no longer had significant commercial success. Rodnitzky writes that of all the activist movements that found support in music, the one with the greatest staying power was the women's movement. He concludes that protest music is the best way to understand the 1960s. Rodnitzky is a professor of history at the University of Texas at Arlington and the author of several books, including *Minstrels of the Dawn: The Folksinger as a Cultural Hero*.

■

Excerpted from "The Sixties Between the Microgrooves: Using Folk and Protest Music to Understand American History, 1963–1973," by Jerome L. Rodnitzky, *Popular Music and Society*, Winter 1999. Reprinted by permission of Bowling Green State University Popular Press.

FOR THOSE TRYING TO FIND AMERICAN HISTORY in its topical music, the 1960s were (with apologies to Charles Dickens) the best of times and the worst of times. The best part was how directly music was tied to social change and how emotionally close Americans were to sixties music. The worst aspect involves sifting through the largest profusion of topical music before or since, to find what really characterized the 1960s. There's little agreement on whose music to center on, once you get past a few icons such as folk legends Bob Dylan and Phil Ochs. There is also little agreement on what folk music is. Perhaps Pete Seeger got as close as anyone did. When asked to define folk music, Seeger replied: "If folks sing them, they're folksongs."

One now can at least find relative agreement that the sixties decade occurred historically (if not chronologically) from 1963 to 1973, rather than from 1960 to 1970. The sixties started slow and ended slow, but topical music kept the beat. Although pacifist and antiwar music wound down with the Vietnam War after 1970, feminist and ecology music just hit their stride in 1973, while backlash against the 1960s counterculture accelerated until the Watergate hearings. Throughout every decade since the sixties, however, music continued its mesmerizing grip on American youth. Frank Zappa said it best in 1967 when he noted that many youths were loyal to neither "flag, country or doctrine, but only to music."

Folk music led the way toward relevant 1960s music. Protest songs were always a part of American folk music, and showcasing them within the entire folk spectrum gave them a wholesome image. In this all-American guise, folksingers invaded the musical vacuum on college campuses during the late 1950s. While jazz had become increasingly complex and abstract and rock-and-roll had become more nonsensical and meaningless, folk songs were filled with meaning and integrity.

Songs About Civil Rights

The 1960s brought events that called folk guitarists to arms and the civil rights movement was the catalyst. Martin Luther King's movement was clearly a sing-in as well as a sit-in campaign. While black Southern activists wrote new songs and "We Shall Overcome" became the civil rights anthem, Northern folksingers developed leaders and anthems of their own. Performer-composers such as Bob Dylan and Phil Ochs recorded both general and specific songs against discrimination, the arms race, and the military-industrial establishment. Song titles such as Ochs's "I Ain't Marching Anymore" and Dylan's "Talking World War Three Blues" suggested common concerns. . . .

The earliest civil rights songs supported protests against segregation. Pete Seeger was the central figure here, and the best emotional feel for the movement comes from his Carnegie Hall concert in June 1963. This live concert recording features songs such as "If You Miss Me at the Back of the Bus," "Keep Your Eyes on the Prize," "I Ain't Scared of Your Jail," "Oh Freedom," and of course, his audience-participation, concert-closing rendition of "We Shall Overcome." These songs were written by various activist-songwriters, both white and black. Some had been taught how to write topical songs at the Highlander Folk School in Tennessee by Seeger and especially by the school director, Guy Carawan. Indeed, "We Shall Overcome" had been remade from a nineteenth-century Baptist hymn and further refined by Carawan and Seeger into the civil rights anthem. Unfortunately, when President Lyndon Johnson proclaimed "We Shall Overcome" in 1964, the song and slogan lost much of its meaning.

In the early 1960s, Bob Dylan also wrote songs with civil rights themes. They were more abstract, but usually more artful. Good examples are his 1963 song "Oxford Town" (about the first black student at the University of Mississippi) and his 1964 ballad "The Lonesome Death of Hattie Carroll" (about the death of a black maid). Many of Dylan's general 1963–64 protest songs vaguely alluded to the civil rights struggle. Good examples are "When the Ship Comes In," "Only a Pawn in Their Game," "The Times They Are a-Changin'," and of course "Blowin' in the Wind." However, in 1965 Dylan suddenly stopped writing protest songs of any kind and about the same time he switched from acoustic to electric guitar. Indeed, Dylan declared his artistic independence from movements and national issues. He made it crystal clear in a remarkable song, "My Back Pages." Here, Dylan proclaimed that he had over-simplified right and wrong in his earlier songs and become what he hated most—a preacher. One line noted that he had convinced himself that "liberty" only constituted "equality in school." However, at the end of each verse, Dylan proclaimed that while he was "older" back then, he was a lot "younger" now.

A Move Toward Universality

Thus, like so many folk music trends, the movement away from specific, topical protest songs was initiated by Bob Dylan, the most creative and influential American performer of the 1960s. Dylan had already pioneered very general protest songs such as "Blowin' in the Wind." In 1965, he merged folk music and rock-and-roll, which the music industry labeled folk-rock. This allowed record companies to merge college and high school markets. This also brought hazy message songs to teenagers and the bestselling singles chart. Throughout the 1960s, folk-rock became heavier and more electric, and those who supported it as teens remained faithful as collegians. In 1965 there was a sudden media hunger for thoughtful songs such as "Universal Soldier," a pacifist song, written by Sioux Indian Buffy Sainte-Marie and recorded by Donovan (The Best of Buffy Ste. Marie), and idiotic songs such as "Eve of Destruction," a thermonuclear warning song recorded by Barry McGuire (Eve of Destruction). Teenagers were now dancing the latest steps to the newest folk-rock, topical songs, and listening to equally new and frantic folk-rock groups such as the Byrds (Turn! Turn! Turn!).

Increasingly, however, the folk-rock protest song radiated general discontent and a vague, anti-establishment mood, as opposed to focusing on specific issues or evils. The protest flavor was still there, and if anything the fervor had increased, yet the lyrics were now less important and often could not be heard clearly over the music anyway. This new psychedelic music registered a protest of form rather than substance. The music often featured sexually explicit lyrics, high creativity, and nonconformist delivery. It presented a hazy but direct protest to white, middle-class America.

Protest songs had been diluted by their success. By 1966, the most popular folk-rock songs of Dylan, Simon and Garfunkel, the Byrds, and others had largely evaporated into an existential haze. By trying to be all things to all people, the songs became universal protest ballads. One could read whatever one wanted into the lines. By saying everything, they in effect said nothing.

The Vietnam War

In 1965, history and the Vietnam War brought America into more dangerous waters. President Lyndon Johnson had accepted the Pentagon's argument that the war could be won with large numbers of American ground troops and massive air power. Whereas discrimination had been harmful to African Americans and embarrassing to the nation, the Vietnam War was lethal to young Americans, black or white. The Southern civil rights issues had been relatively simple to argue; Vietnam was far more complex and divisive. The war merged issues of patriotism, anticommunism, and world peace; and it splintered traditional American political and class alliances. The clearest division on the war was between young and old. Antiwar slogans such as "Make Love, Not War" and "Don't Trust Anyone over 30" were hardly directed toward the old. The war destroyed Johnson's administration and political career; and it left his successor, Richard Nixon, with a war-torn nation.

Although specific protest songs no longer made the Top 40 chart after 1965, a continuing stream of protest songs were written for smaller, specialized groups of activists. Ironically, the Vietnam War accelerated just as the pacifist song "Universal Soldier" became a nationwide hit. And Glen Campbell, who recorded "Universal Soldier," supported the war and was quoted as saying that "anyone who wouldn't fight for his country was no real man." Later that year the California-based rock duo Jan and Dean parodied "Universal Soldier" in a song titled "Universal Coward," about a coward who ran "from Uncle Sam" and ran "from Vietnam." However, as the antiwar movement grew, songwriters such as Phil Ochs, Pete Seeger, and Tom Paxton led the way with very specific anti-Vietnam protest songs. They also encouraged a host of younger protest songwriters.

Perhaps the most famous antiwar song was Pete Seeger's "Waist Deep in the Big Muddy." It told the story of a 1942 Army platoon being pushed by a captain to ford a dangerously deep river. The punch line noted that "the big fool" told his men "to push on." It was clearly a parable about the Vietnam War and the "big fool" was obviously Lyndon Johnson. Seeger sang the song for a 1967 Smothers Brothers television show, but CBS censored it off the scheduled program, because Seeger refused to omit the last verse, which tied the song to Vietnam and Johnson. In response to protests against network censorship, CBS finally permitted the song to be sung in full on a January 1968 Smothers Brothers show. After the CBS nightly news (anchored by Walter Cronkite) became sharply critical of the Vietnam War in 1968, antiwar censorship on television was much less a problem. Thus, on a 1969 Smothers Brothers show, Seeger was allowed to sing "Bring Them Home," a direct call for America to bring home its troops and to end the war. . . .

Championing Environmental and Feminist Causes

One sixties movement that drew activists from both the Left and the Right in an uneasy alliance was the ecology or environmental movement. While many advocates worked to save wildlife and wetlands, others warned about the environmental pollution hazards to humans. Several folksingers wrote songs about the environment. But some environmental songs just celebrated current natural beauty, rather than warning about future loss. Also, many of the warning songs about nuclear fallout, such as Bob Dylan's 1964 "A Hard Rain's A-Gonna Fall," were tied to antiwar themes. Perhaps the earliest and best of this genre was Malvina Reynolds's much-covered 1963 song "What Have They Done to the Rain." The recording that best combined memories of past natural beauty with apocalyptic visions of possible future ecological destruction was Tom Paxton's 1970 "Whose Garden Was This." A close second would be Billy Edd Wheeler's "The Coming of the Roads" (about the effects of strip mining), beautifully sung by Judy Collins in 1965.

The singer-songwriter who most consistently championed ecological causes was Pete Seeger. Environmental songs appear on most of his albums, and he was a constant environmental activist. Seeger was famous for sailing up and down the Hudson River to publicize efforts to clean that waterway. He also was the first singer to [sing] Woody Guthrie's 1930s tune "This Land Is Your Land" from a socialist political song into the sixties' major ecology anthem. Guthrie's song did highlight America's natural beauty, but his real message was that America belonged to the little people and not just to corporations and politicians. The Seeger album that concentrated most on ecology is God Bless the Grass. This 1966 recording devotes eleven songs to environmental issues, including two Malvina Reynolds pieces— "The Faucets Are Dripping" and "70 Miles." Other highlights are: "The People Are Scratching" (loosely based on Rachel Carson's warning of ecological interdependence in Silent Spring) and Seeger's song "My Dirty Stream" (about his attempts to clean up the Hudson River).

Of all the sixties activist movements, the one with the most staying power, and perhaps the most important, was the women's liberation movement. The feminist movement was also the most divisive, since it largely excluded males. Topical music was particularly useful to young feminists, who followed the New Left maxim of organizing around your own oppression. Furthermore, since feminism pioneered consciousness raising, what better device to accomplish this than topical songs? Women's liberation music is very diverse—ranging from workers' songs to ballads of cultural pride and psychological independence. Compared to the previous women's movement—the suffrage movement—the new mood was much more strident and the goals much more fundamental. Early 1960s feminist songs such as "The Modern Union Maid," a parody of Guthrie's 1936 ballad about wives of union men, "Stand and Be Counted" (a marching song), "The Freedom Ladies," with its firm but humorous declaration of independence, and "Papa," a put-down of sexist male rock musicians by the Chicago Women's Liberation Rock Band are all adept at capturing the verve and complexity of the early feminist movement. The first feminist singers were usually obscure groups of rather amateur musicians, but they often made up for musical weaknesses with their spirit and sisterly solidarity. More polished individual feminist singers would emerge in the early 1970s.

Actually, women folksingers who did not identify with feminism, such as Joan Baez, Judy Collins, and Malvina Reynolds, were excellent feminist role models in the 1960s. They often sang songs about independent, aggressive women

A Watershed Year

If music by itself were capable of destroying social foundations, jazz, which represented values and sensibilities alien to most Americans, would have played that role long before 1964. Yet the whirlwind of emotion let loose by the Beatles' arrival and the spread of Motown reflected a cultural explosion that had a recurring social impact.

In 1964 conditions conspired to create an ambience for change. There was the emergence into adolescence of the first wave of baby boomers. A "youth culture" was manufactured with its own "needs" and pandered to with overheated political rhetoric. There were the emotional peaks of Kennedy's election and the low of his assassination. There were students everywhere; *more people went to schools, colleges, and universities in the sixties than in any other decade in American history.* There was fat-dripping, split-level, convertible-hopping affluence on an unprecedented scale. There was an election in 1964 in which the candidate who was elected talked of a "Great Society," the "quality of life," and a "war on poverty." And hanging over the society of 1964 were the dark and ominous clouds of a war in Vietnam, a war that had American advisors but had not yet created an uproar at home. Vietnam was to become to this revolution in sensibilities what World War I was to the Russian Revolution. It was lighter fluid put on the fire. The Germans use the proverb, "The soup is never eaten as hot as it's cooked." But by the end of the decade, many were force fed with boiling hot soup. And the Vietnam war seemed to be the fire on which the soup was boiling.

By the end of the decade, this nation was in the midst of a psychological reign of terror. In 1964, however, one could only sense what would happen.

Herbert I. London, *Closing the Circle: A Cultural History of the Rock Revolution*, 1984.

and they ably competed with the best male topical singers. They predated women's liberation—a term first used in 1968. There was a women's movement in the early 1960s—dating either from John Kennedy's Federal Commission on the Status of Women in 1960 or from Betty Friedan's 1963 publication of *The Feminine Mystique*. However, the women's liberation movement originated in 1966 when young "New Left" activist college women split from male-dominated radical groups such as SNCC (Student Nonviolent Coordinating Committee) and SDS (Students for a Democratic Society).

These younger feminists completely transformed the early 1960s women's movement, with its stress on equal rights, into a diverse countercultural movement that concentrated on capturing and changing the next generation of men and women. . . . These feminists had also grown up with protest songs, but since they had separated from the New Left just as topical music declined, they escaped the malaise. Feminist songwriters felt everything they wrote broke new ground. Whether they performed traditional songs, wrote topical ballads, or wrote about their own experiences, they felt they were speaking to the conditions of all women. Women's liberation greatly encouraged women songwriters. In 1976 the introduction to *All Our Lives: A Women's Songbook* summed up the fruits of the past decade: "As women and as feminists who love folk music and who love to sing, we have produced this book as a reflection of our own struggles in a society which still has so little room for a woman with a mind of her own—even less for a woman with a song of her own.". . .

On balance, early women's liberation music was far better than one would expect. Art and politics are often joined, but seldom compatible; and women's liberation music was necessarily political. Yet political mission often fuels the imagination, while audience enthusiasm can provide creative incentives. Considering the political pressures, the most surprising thing about the early feminist movement and its music was its diversity. Feminist critics sometimes patronized women who made music in traditional ways—with acoustic guitars or piano accompaniment. The big challenge was proving that women could play rock and that hard rock need not be sexist to be good. But the best feminist music largely followed women's traditional musical forms and the traditional feminist singers were not put down in practice. For one thing, the women's movement stressed the need to support all women artists. For another, feminists realized the potential that quality feminist music offered for making new recruits think seriously about the women's movement. The traditional women the movement hoped to attract were more likely to seriously consider a subtle, sensitive, well-done ballad than a second-rate, derivative rock number. The woman rock musician (Bonnie Raitt or Joan Jett, for example) would later get more attention, but often drew attention to themselves at the expense of their music. Feminism had quickly concluded that the real power of music was its ability to communicate rather than its ability to shock or cross male boundaries. A host of effective feminist singer-songwriters, such as Willie Tyson, Meg Christian, and Kristin Lems, would follow the example of the pioneer feminist singers. . . .

Music Helps Explain the Decade

With its special connection to youth, rock music became and remains an important cultural early warning system. Like the more specific protest music of the era, it brings back the mood and mania of the 1960s and its counterculture. Thus, if there was a political or social counterculture in the 1960s, surely it lived between the microgrooves of both rock and topical records. Music is still the best guide to understanding a decade that some historians will continue to label "the Age of Protest."

The Demise of Political Rock in the 1970s

John Orman

The political overtones of music in the 1960s began to fade away in the 1970s. John Orman details the death of political rock in the 1970s in the following essay. Trends such as disco, women's rock, and country rock began to overshadow the political music that had been created by MC5 and other 1960s bands. According to Orman, the revolutionary aspect of rock music was replaced by a desire to make money. Orman is a history professor at Fairfield University in Fairfield, Connecticut, and the author of *The Politics of Rock Music*, the source of the following article.

MANY THOUGHT THAT ROCK MUSIC COULD BE A tool for a real revolution in America. Jim Morrison said: "Erotic politicians, that's what we are. We're interested in anything about revolt, disorder, chaos and activity that appears to have no meaning." For some, rock would create a social revolution in consciousness. In this spirit, Country Joe McDonald observed, "The most revolutionary thing you can do in this country is change your mind."

Two Approaches to Rock and Politics

Two rock groups in particular started out specifically to be "rock and revolution" groups, but only one made it commercially. These groups were the MC5 and Chicago. The MC5

■

were managed by White Panther John Sinclair. They had their own brand of hard-driving rock that "kicked out the jams," but they failed to gain a mass audience. As rock critic Ben Fong-Torres noted, "They wanted to be bigger than the Beatles; he [John Sinclair] wanted them to be bigger than Mao."

MC5 was part of the Ann Arbor (Michigan) politico-social scene, and their audiences were mostly composed of "street people" and "freaks." In the early 1970s, after Sinclair was busted for marijuana possession, the group began having serious problems. Their new manager, rock critic Jon Landau, wanted them to drop all their political rhetoric and become a cultural force within the rock industry. Yet the band was caught in a dilemma. If they compromised their political positions so they could be commercially successful, then they would lose their original following. The fact that their best album sold only 100,000 copies did the MC5 in. Though some rock critics thought they were a new, great force in music, the mass audience had problems with rock and revolution. The MC5 quickly became the "George McGovern" of political rock and faded away.

The rock group Chicago, which was originally called Chicago Transit Authority or CTA, became one of the most commercially successful groups ever to record. Even though Chicago started out as a "rock and revolution" band, it was never really clear whether the group was politically active early on because producer James William Guercio thought activism would sell or because they were sincere. Chicago had a big rock-jazz band sound, replete with horns, that sold more than forty million albums for the group in 1974. For the mass rock audience, Chicago was clearly doing something right. Yet after their first two albums, the politics of the group began to disappear.

Chicago's first album contained tributes to the Chicago anti-war demonstrations at the Chicago Democratic national convention in 1968, including some live recordings of the street confrontations between police and demonstrators in a song called "Liberation." The second Chicago album was dedicated to "the people of the revolution . . . and the revolution in all its forms." For many activists it was absurd for Chicago to sing about revolution when they were making millions of dollars on each album and not filtering the money back into the movement. In effect, Chicago profited from the movement ethos. Later, in 1972, to show how revolutionary they had become, the group started pushing voter registration for young people. They supported George McGovern for the presidency and did some work to raise money for him. This was hardly the radical critique of society that some people thought Chicago had promised.

McGovern's defeat in 1972 ended the group's participation in politics, except for a post-Watergate tune about the need for Harry Truman to return to the presidency. Chicago retired on their beautiful Caribou ranch in Colorado for the rest of the 1970s, making albums and millions of dollars. One way to get back to the land, they found, was to buy it! Lead singer Robert Lamm summed up his political involvement in the 1970s: "At the time [1972] I really gave a shit, but I don't anymore. If McGovern could lose by that margin, then I and everybody I know must be nothing."

Perhaps the incident that best portrayed the problems of combining rock and revolution in the United States came when Peter Townshend of the Who hit Abbie Hoffman over the head with his guitar at Woodstock in 1969. Hoffman wanted to turn the Woodstock Nation on to some radical political ideas during the Who's set, and Townshend indicated where his priorities were by bashing away at Hoffman. Later Townshend would write one of his best songs, "Won't Get Fooled Again," that warned people not to follow the now revolutionary leaders and the rhetoric of the movement because everyone got fooled by those leaders and gurus in the 1960s. Townshend hoped that people would not get fooled again. Ironically, Townshend became a spiritual rock guru for many people in the 1970s, precisely the sort of thing that he had spoken out against in the early 1970s and in his 1960s rock opera *Tommy*.

By most accounts, the experience of rock and revolution in the United States was a failure. Rock failed to gain converts for the so-called revolution and the revolution "in all its forms" did not seem to be scoring the kinds of successes that a revolution needs to sustain itself.

The demise of political rock came after the May Day demonstrations in Washington, D.C., in 1971, and this reflected an end to an era of protest. Rock music was not politicized during the great commercial successes of the rock industry in the so-called "me decade" of the 1970s.

Rock music continued to branch out in new directions—theatrical rock, glitter rock, black superstar pop rock, disco, jazz, country, southern rock, art rock, women's rock, and LA rock, to name a few. The Watergate crisis should have been covered in many rock songs; instead, there was almost no response by rock poets. Lynyrd Skynyrd captured this feeling in "Sweet Home Alabama" (1974) when listeners were asked if Watergate bothered them, the implication being that it clearly didn't bother the band. Only such popular acts as Neil Young and Arlo Guthrie showed any understanding of the Watergate affair in their songs.

Post-Watergate rock in the 1970s lacked excitement for the most part. Rock concerts had become so ritualized that few people went to them to actually listen to the music, rather they went "to make the scene." Matches were ignited at the right time to call for encores, even if the groups were performing their songs in poor fashion. Rock developed into a "monster out of control" in the 1970s as the prices of concerts and albums more than kept pace with inflation. For many acts, artistry vanished; money was the only name of the game. Companies and artists searched for "monster" albums like *Peter Frampton Comes Alive*, Fleetwood Mac's *Rumours*, the soundtrack of *Saturday Night Fever*, or Carole King's *Tapestry*. The institutionalization of rock music came about in the 1970s as rock developed a set of standard operating procedures within popular culture. The key idea for the artist was to be "safe" and not to take chances. Yet, as Jon Landau has observed about rock, "It's too late to stop now!"

The 1970s saw the glitter-rock culture, which owed a debt to the gay liberation movement of the early 1970s and the influences of Mick Jagger and Ray Davies (Kinks) in the 1960s. David Bowie, Alice Cooper, the New York Dolls, and a host of other glitter rockers made ambisexual poses on stage complete with make-up and feminine fashions. As rock philosopher Frank Zappa once said, "We're only in it for the money!"

Another trend in the 1970s saw the black artist finally getting some big bucks by taking to the middle-of-the-road, middle-class pop market. Stevie Wonder, Al Green, the Com-

modores, Marvin Gaye, and Michael Jackson all made significant sales to the young pop-rock masses. In some circles, Stevie Wonder was recognized as *the* pop artist of the 1970s. Sly
and the Family Stone and Jimi Hendrix had been influential
with white audiences from 1967 to 1971, but Wonder sur-
passed their influence in the 1970s. Black artists had been denied big profits in rock music for many years, though white
artists often used black trends to make a profit. Finally, with
the success of disco in the mid-1970s, many more black artists
were able to share some of the rock 'n' roll money. This helped
in some small way to reverse a trend that Immamu Amiri
Baraka (LeRoi Jones) had noted about white rockers: they
stole from blacks and kept all the money.

New Trends Emerged

The Byrds, Bob Dylan, and Neil Young started a down-home,
back-to-nature, plain shirt, heart-of-gold, and cabin-in-Utah
brand of rock in the late 1960s and early 1970s. In the remaining years of the 1970s, Jackson Browne, James Taylor,
and Neil Young continued the tradition. Other country rock
groups, like the Eagles, became superstars with their brand of
Los Angeles-country-desert rock. Country rock branched out
into southern rock, led by the Allman Brothers Band, the Marshall Tucker Band, Lynyrd Skynyrd, and the Charlie Daniels
Band. The mountain minstrel was represented in the pop field
by John Denver. The country rock explosion also allowed real
country-and-western artists to become stars in the world of
rockdom—Waylon Jennings, Willie Nelson, and Dolly Parton. And washed-up rock acts like Kenny Rogers crossed over
into the field of country music to score amazing successes.

The infusion of great jazz artists into the rock market
also took place in the 1970s with artists like Herbie Han-
cock, Miles Davis, John McLaughlin, Billy Cobham, and
Chick Corea leading the way. Young record buyers were inspired to go back and pick up on earlier jazz greats like
Charlie Parker, Pharoah Sanders, John Coltrane, Ornette
Coleman, and Thelonious Monk.

The female rock singer finally had her day in the 1970s,
even though rock music essentially was still a sexist institution.
Joni Mitchell, Carole King, Carly Simon, Bonnie Raitt, Bette

Midler, and particularly Linda Ronstadt sold many records and received critical acclaim. In the 1960s, other than the black soul singers and the "girl groups," women in rock had been limited to Grace Slick and Janis Joplin. The 1970s saw women taking an independent role and scoring as solo acts. Other acts like Heart, led by Nancy and Ann Wilson, and Pat Benatar scored impressive hits in the 1970s. Middle-of-the-road female pop singers like Olivia Newton-John, Marie Osmond, Anne Murray, Karen Carpenter, and Helen Reddy sold records in the rock market also.

Perhaps the most significant trend of the middle 1970s in rock was the tremendous popularity of disco. Disco broke into the mainstream with songs by Donna Summer, Gloria Gaynor, the Bee Gees, and the Village People. Summer emerged as the queen of disco, and later crossed over into the rock and soul market. Disco created an alternative culture to the remnants of the rock and dope cultures of the 1960s. The disco culture stressed whirling dance lights, fashionable designer jeans, and monotonous, computerized, loud synthetic music that did not require the listener to think at all.

But of all these trends, none except the punk rock/new wave movement could be considered political. Mostly they reflected a dissatisfaction with rock and politics and represented a retreat from sociopolitical stances of the 1960s and 1970s. Only a few rock artists had been political from 1967 to 1971, and as these artists began their retreat in the "me decade" of introspection and self-improvement, the political content of rock turned into an apathetic stance.

The Impact of Feminism on Rock Music in the 1970s and 1980s

Mavis Bayton

In the following essay, Mavis Bayton explains how feminists in the 1970s created a new type of music that reflected their political views. According to Bayton, these women stood apart from their male counterparts lyrically and musically; the lyrics tended to focus on issues such as motherhood and lesbianism, while the music was generally lighter and softer. Feminist musicians also emphasized cooperation between each other and between the performer and the audience. Bayton is a tutor in sociology at Ruskin College in Oxford, England. She has also written numerous articles on rock music and is the author of *Frock Rock: Women Performing Popular Music.*

EXCLUDED FROM THE MAINSTREAM (MALE) ROCK world, 1970s feminists created an alternative musical world of their own. This world offered the chance to rewrite the rules: of lyrics, of band membership and organization, of the gig, of the stage, and even of the music itself. Feminists enthusiastically and optimistically promoted alternative values: collectivism and cooperation instead of competitive individualism; participative democracy and equality instead of hierarchy. The general feminist belief that 'the personal is political', derived

■

Excerpted from "Feminist Musical Practice: Problems and Contradictions," by Mavis Bayton, in *Rock and Popular Music: Politics, Policies, and Institutions*, edited by Tony Bennett et al. Copyright ©1993 Tony Bennett, Simon Frith, Lawrence Grossberg, John Shepherd, and Graeme Turner. Reprinted by permission of Routledge.

from the American students' movement, when transposed into rock worked to break down the barriers between band life and 'personal' life. The 'professionalism' of the typical male band was rejected in favour of an approach which minimized the boundary between the band and the rest of women's lives. Some of the early feminist bands were often variants of women's groups in the general sense, deliberately engaging in consciousness-raising as well as playing music together. Jean recalls her first experience in a feminist band back in 1976:

> 'We met once a week and we used to talk after every rehearsal. We were all really eager to talk to each other. We just used to talk and talk and talk. We just used to sit around the table and it was amazing. . . . We used to take turns. It became more like a consciousness-raising thing as well as a band. We were really close.'

The politics of the personal was also reflected in the need to write alternative lyrics. Women have written about topics not generally appropriated to popular music: menstruation, housework, lesbianism, motherhood, the menopause. Most women have preferred to write their own numbers rather than do (male) 'standards' and, indeed, songwriting has become normative for feminist bands. If covers are performed, they are invariably altered and subverted—'he' becomes 'she', and so on. Love songs become especially politicized.

Establishing Musical Relationships

The belief that one's methods of work tend to affect the product has led to attempts for band-members to interact within bands in new ways. For example, 'showing off' is considered to be deviant whereas in male music-making it is normative. Some feminist performers have gone to great lengths in order to avoid being seen as special or different from their 'sisters' in the audience, as Angela recalled:

> 'When we first started the band, we found certain things very difficult. Like, we weren't sure whether we should play on a stage, and we weren't sure about having lights on us, and we didn't think the audience should be in darkness. . . . There's definitely a differentiation I've never been able to quite come

to grips with: the whole thing between the audience and the group. Because you can't really get into this thing of "we're all here together enjoying ourselves", because it's not quite like that . . . they've actually paid to see you and you're getting paid for playing. You're in a different position.'

Feminist musicians have been concerned with the quality of their relationships, as well as with their music. Co-operation is stressed, as is giving each other space for expression and trying not to put other women down. Bands have had political policies on the manual labour of 'roadying' and 'setting up', insisting that everyone should do it equally.

Rock bands are structurally pitched into competition with each other for gigs, for financial rewards, and for acclaim by the press and public. Bands on the same 'bill' are, conventionally, competing for status. Many people who go to gigs tend to miss the first ('support') acts and only turn up to see the 'main band'. Some feminist bands have tried to abolish the 'headlining' problem by rotating the order of play between the bands. For example, Jean (guitarist in a well-established jazz-influenced band on the women's circuit) commented:

'We got fed up with this "Who's supporting?" and "Who's headlining?" And we say, "As far as the women's movement's concerned, that's just straight shit! What we're gonna do is take it in turns." And that's what we've done ever since. . . . I really think that these are discussions that we have really prompted in the women's movement, that people really don't think about. They're really political in other aspects of their life, but when it comes to music they're really blocked. Any time we've organized gigs, this has been going on behind the scenes. . . . Any bands that we come in contact with get told the same thing, and few of them disagree. . . . That's how you deal with your sisters.'

These feminist ideals are not simply imprinted on band practice but they are aspired to, and translated into everyday life to varying degrees. Inevitably there are contradictions and tensions and these have to be negotiated and lived. Furthermore, feminist music ideology has, to a degree, drawn on other alternative forms of musical discourse. Some of these cultural beliefs and practices have been common to punk, left-wing and anarchist bands. Indeed, such cross-fertilization is inevitable. But feminist music is largely the offspring of feminism in general, spawned in the heady political days of the late 1960s. My argument here is twofold. First, feminism, both as a route into music-making and as an alternative music discourse, has been underexamined compared with the predominantly male alternative forms of punk and left-wing music. Second, feminist music practice has, in some ways, been more radical than these other forms. For example, for feminists, 'personal politics' meant that children were brought to practices and gigs. It was unheard of for male musicians to do this, even those in 'political' bands. Indeed, it is still uncommon.

Like punks, feminists have rewritten the rules of public performance; they have challenged the spatial norms of the gig. They have treated their audiences differently, and gigs have been physically transformed. But they have done this in a different way from punk bands. By speaking and singing to the women in the audience—by prioritizing them—feminist bands have challenged the traditional taken-for-granted dominance of men at gigs. For example, Anne (keyboard player in an all-women 'power-pop' band, 1978–81) said:

> 'One thing I've found, women at mixed gigs tend to come up to the front. So the people who can actually see you are women. . . . And I very much talk to the women. I play to the women, definitely . . . because women have been ignored by rock music, generally, apart from just as sex objects, and it's nice to treat them differently.' . . .

Music and Gender Roles

As the 1970s wore on, the 'Women's Liberation Movement' became 'the women's movement' and then the term 'feminism' subsumed them both.

The movement was growing and, in the process, fragmenting. Many varieties of feminism were sprouting up. In the late 1970s the development of revolutionary feminism signalled a move away from the early strategy of breaking into men's terrain and towards separatism. Within popular music, this reinforced the development of alternative institutional structures.

At the same time, however, radical separatism buttressed

an 'essentialist' world view which had important ramifications for feminist music-making. Certain styles of music were deemed to be intrinsically 'male' and thus inappropriate terrain for feminist musicians. Some feminists considered all electric music to be 'male', because of its loudness and the way in which the panoply of amplification devices distances the performers from the audience.

The consequent attempts positively to define a 'female' music proved to be impossible. It was far easier to specify what 'women's music' was not: loud, noisy, driving 'cock rock'. Thus, so-called female music had to be lighter and softer. But, beyond that, there was little agreement. Sarah (vocalist and percussionist in a feminist pop band which formed in 1979) suggested that:

> 'It's less heavy, less throbbing . . . there's a concern for lyrics to be heard and not just a technological slur.'

Kate (guitarist/vocalist/keyboard player in a mixed post-punk band which formed in 1980) felt that:

> 'Female music's a bit warmer. It tends to be less rock'n'roll. Women play less aggressively, generally. They caress it more, and men rock it and slap it. Women tend to like off-beat rhythms. That's why it's rare to find a women's rock'n'roll band.'

The problem was that so much music had been labelled 'male' that only the folk area was considered ideologically safe. Paradoxically, then, the feminist challenge looked likely to result in retreat from rock and amplified music altogether.

Moreover, descriptions of music slid easily into discussions of performance, instead. For instance, Pat (guitarist in the same band as Sarah) expressed the view that:

> 'Well, all male music isn't, presumably, about wanking off on your instrument, but I think quite a lot of it is. And, maybe, competing with other players in the band—obviously, women's music isn't like that. . . . It's definitely a thing apart.'

Of all styles of music, 'heavy metal' has been viewed as the epitome of 'maleness' and only a tiny minority of women have played in this musical style. In the early 1980s there were no more than half a dozen all-women heavy metal bands in the whole of the UK. I interviewed members of one of these bands. Aware of the criticisms, they adamantly defended their right to play in this genre and saw no contradiction between playing heavy metal and feminism. Eva felt that:

'A lot of people see heavy metal as being very aggressive, [but] I don't see myself as being very aggressive, really. I love all that racket. A lot of women . . . tend to play very sort of ethereal music, very spiritual. I like physical, lusty, earthy, passionate music. I was at a rhythm workshop a while back, and the woman who was taking it described the 4/4 snare drum beat as a white, male, militaristic, fascist, patriarchal rhythm, and I think that's a bit heavy, man! . . . Is there any such thing as female music and male music? I don't know. Women are seen as more intuitive, and I don't think this is a natural phenomenon. I think women and men have equal capacity for logic and rationality, and an equal capacity for intuition.'

For feminists who took this position, what was important was how the noise was used—what the songs were about, for example. That is what demarcated feminist heavy rock from 'male' heavy rock.

This debate, which came to the boil in the early 1980s and which still lingers on, is an interesting manifestation of the wider contradiction within feminism of, on the one hand, wanting to do what men do, and, on the other, wanting to create something altogether different, which expresses women's 'femaleness'. This is currently called the 'sameness/difference' or 'equality-difference' debate.

Women who strongly resist the notion that women should play quieter, gentler music argue that it is based on the sexist stereotype of conventional femininity. For such women, it is bad enough male musicians and male audiences telling them that they should not (or cannot) play heavy rock, without feminists reiterating the message. If all existing ways of playing and being on stage were rejected as being 'male', then there would be very little space for women to manoeuvre.

Musical essentialism lives on in some quarters, but it is no longer an orthodoxy, having been strongly challenged by women who wanted to make loud powerful music and bitterly resented the expectation that, as feminists, they should restrict themselves to being 'spiritual'. Women's liberation had been associated with the freedom of women to express themselves, but more recent feminism seemed, to many women, to be about prohibition. It was, above all, punk feminists like Veronica who protested these views and kept women musicians on the rock stage:

> 'It took a year before I turned my guitar volume up . . . because I was still scared of it, of making a noise to that extent. I turned the knobs down on my guitar for a whole year. And, then, suddenly I thought, "Fuck it. I'm not going to do that anymore." . . . I get a buzz out of handling big energy and I think it can be subverted. . . . I've learnt how to make a big noise only recently, and I like it. And I'm not going to be told by any boy that I'm on their preserves and get off! . . . I don't feel that because I've got a big voice I'm any less of a woman. . . . I mean, a woman lion can roar just as loud as a male lion. . . . For me it's undercutting a whole lot of conditioning. . . . And, I believe, collectively, women have a right to this. . . . I feel it's some sort of celebration of something very animal and basic. . . . I understand the function of men making a lot of noise. . . . What I object to is that they do it on our backs, and at our expense, and keep us out. That's why the opposite of saying "Get off our territory!" is; I want *every* woman who wants to make a big noise to get on with it too.'

The question of what type of music should be performed, then, highlights some of the key paradoxes of contemporary feminism: 'It acknowledges diversity among women while positing that women recognize their unity. It requires gender consciousness for its basis, yet calls for the elimination of prescribed gender roles'.

Feminism Is a Musical Force

There are very few professional all-women bands, indeed there is a limited number of professional women instrumentalists in general. This is a reflection, in the main, of the narrow base from which they develop: the small number of women taking up rock instruments. I have found that gender constraints operate most strongly in the early stages of women's musical careers, and it is then that feminism has its major impact.

Despite its inherent contradictions, feminism has been a major force in getting women into popular music-making. It has given women access to instruments and provided safe women-only spaces for the learning of skills as well as rehearsal and performance; it has challenged ingrained 'technophobia' and given women the confidence to believe that, like the boys, they can be music-makers rather than simply music fans. Feminism has been a long-lasting oppositional and enabling force within popular music.

The Anti-Conformity Ethos of Punk Rock

Craig O'Hara

In the following selection, Craig O'Hara writes that the punk movement stands in opposition to the conformity of mainstream rock and roll. The punk movement, particularly in Britain, originally consisted largely of underprivileged and working-class adolescents who were angry about their bleak social and economic prospects. According to O'Hara, punks spoke out against authority and conformity, questioning the prevailing views of society. However, as the punk movement gained in popularity, it began to receive acceptance from the society that had first scorned it. O'Hara is the author of *The Philosophy of Punk: More than Noise*, which he originally wrote as a graduate student at Boston University.

"In a mechanical and depersonalized world man has an indefinable sense of loss; a sense that life . . . has become impoverished, that men are somehow 'deracinate and disinherited,' that society and human nature alike have been atomized, and hence mutilated, above all that men have been separated from whatever might give meaning to their work and their lives" (Charles Taylor as quoted in *Man Alone*, edited by Eric and Mary Josephson, Dell Publishing New York, 1962, 11).

∎

THERE IS A CURRENT FEELING IN MODERN SOCI-
ety of an alienation so powerful and widespread that it has become commonplace and accepted. Some trace its roots to the
beginnings of the Industrial Revolution when the work place
became a second home for young and old alike. It does not
take a Marxist or a learned sociologist to realize the role of
mass production and maximum efficiency in creating alienation. The peculiar part is that man has been the one who created, agreed to, and accepted these feelings as normal. Perhaps
we cannot remember a time without such feelings and that we
are now merely inheriting the negative structures which cause
alienation. Few can argue with the idea that "Western man
(and increasingly Eastern as well) has become mechanized,
routinized, made comfortable as an object; but in the profound
sense displaced and thrown off balance as a subjective creator
and power."

Responding to Alienation

Human beings act as if they have nothing in common with each
other. It is as if we have all been brought here to function for
ourselves in a way that does not include others. Many philoso-
phers, sociologists, and theologians have attempted to show the
ridiculousness of the atomistic, alienated lifestyles we have cho-
sen. While the intellectual community has often shown the
ability to see the "big picture" of how things really are, this insight has mostly been kept to themselves in academic publications and confined to institutions of higher education.

Occasionally, however, a group of the alienated will recognize what is happening to themselves. This realization can be
based on an active rejection either of or by the mainstream society. These groups can either reject the alienation they see
before them or can be unwillingly alienated from the mainstream. Blacks, homosexuals, HIV+, the lower classes, etc., all
have been brought together by either the realization of hierar-
chies or forced together by an active hierarchy. It is important
to note that the realization of one's own group, or self, being
an "out-group" does not entail the realization of other out-
groups suffering under the same treatment. People have often
woken up to see the details of their own suffering while still
maintaining ignorance to the suffering of others.

Some out-groups greatly desire to be a part of the mainstream while others do not. Nevertheless, "all such out-groups face a certain degree of isolation from society; they are in the community but not of it. As a result, they tend to form more or less distinct 'subcultures' of their own." These subcultures appear to have members who are much less alienated from their own being and often trying to reclaim their subjective powers. Members of subcultures, regardless of how oppressed, have often succeeded in finding a solidarity and understanding amongst themselves that is lacking in mainstream society. Members seem to regain a sense of themselves and each other that had been previously lost, forgotten, or stolen. This is seen in the emergence of support groups based on shared experiences, beliefs, sex or race. What subcultures can succeed in doing is "to imbue their members with some sense of higher purpose." This higher purpose is not always positive as in cases such as the KKK or other hate group subcultures, but is an important component to have in any movement desiring to make changes in the status quo.

The subculture of Rock and Roll music has been an unsteady and complicated one to define. It seems idealistic and unlikely that Rock music (having started a number of years before Elvis Presley and continuing in its many forms today) has had any higher purpose than to entertain. Rebellious youths have been drawn to its changing forms for four decades, but as a whole it has been merely another part of the ever growing entertainment industry. Early Rock and Roll vaguely addressed the racial barriers and inequalities of the fifties, but it was not until the late sixties that distinct politics were carried in Rock music. It was at this time that Rock showed its power and the subculture became a counterculture.

"In the sixties, Rock became the soundtrack for the youth counterculture and helped galvanize resistance to the Vietnam war." Whatever good this music served by giving praises to freedom and disdain for social hypocrisy, it met the same fate as all earlier and later forms of popular Rock: "commercial dilution/creative exhaustion, co-option and takeover by mainstream forces." Rock music became "either commodified, mainstream music promoted and packaged by corporate giants, or ritual, shallow hedonism."

An exception to Rock and Roll's predictable mainstream politics and actions has been the movement called Punk Rock, or simply Punk. The time and birthplace of the Punk movement is debatable. Either the New York scene of the late sixties/early seventies or the British Punks of 1975–76 can be given the honor. For our purposes neither one deserves a long investigation as the specific politics and genuine forming of a movement was not until the late seventies. In general it is thought that the New Yorkers invented the musical style while the British popularized the political attitude and colorful appearances. A quick look at the background of the English scene will show the circumstances in which modern Punk was born.

Tricia Henry has written a very good book which docu-

The Music of the Ramones

Bill Osgerby examines the lyrics and image of the Ramones, one of the most influential bands to come out of the late 1970s New York punk scene.

Standard-bearers of CBGB's punk vanguard, the Ramones took the Dictators' gleeful, cartoon-like parody of American adolescent culture to new extremes. Borrowing an alias used by Paul McCartney in his early Beatles days, band members (Johnny, Joey, Tommy, Dee Dee and later Marky, Ritchie, C.J. and—for one brief, fleeting moment—Elvis) adopted the surname 'Ramone' as a source of unity. The 'Ramone' appellation, however, could also be read as a jokey play on the schmaltzy sibling groups of the 60s and early 70s—the Osmonds, the Partridge Family and the Jackson Five. "Da brudders" outfits of battered leather jackets, ragged drain-pipe jeans and soiled sneakers also wryly echoed the twee uniforms favoured by the early Beatles, the Beach Boys and the Monkees. But whereas these 60s teen favourites had the image of fresh-faced and loveable 'boys next door', the Ramones proudly cultivated the image of geeky losers—as Johnny Ramone was later to

ments the beginnings of the Punk movement in New York and its subsequent rise in England. While the book is good, it ignores everything done since 1980, when she considers Punk to have died. Several books of this kind have been written (all concentrating on the largest of all Punk bands, the Sex Pistols) and most lack a great deal of information, as they were done by writers who were not part of the movement, but outside interpreters. Henry is, however, correct and thorough on the subject at hand.

For the large number of people on welfare—or 'the dole,' as it is known in Great Britain—especially young people, the outlook for bettering their lot in life seemed bleak. In this atmosphere, when the English were exposed to the seminal

quip: 'We wanted to write songs about cars and girls—but none of us had a car and no girls wanted to go out with us. So we wrote about freaks and mental illness instead'.

The Ramones drew lyrical inspiration from the most tawdry corners of American trash culture. References to cheap drugs, delinquency, side-show freaks and lurid horror comics punctuated songs like 'Cretin Hop', 'Chain Saw' and 'Beat on the Brat'. Yet this was always underpinned by a knowing sense of dark humour. As Dee Dee Ramone once sniggered when quizzed on the wisdom of writing a song like 'Now I Wanna Sniff Some Glue':

It's good for you. It expands your mind (laughter). Now we're all successful, happy people (laughter). . . . It was funny, though. 'Now I Wanna Sniff Some *Glue'—Nobody* would write a song like that. We thought it was *hysterically* funny.

The Ramones' universe was always distinguished by a droll duality. Alongside their smirking caricatures of the dire fears lurking in the basement of the suburban consciousness, the Ramones also blissfully celebrated all the clichés and stereotypes of American teen mythology.

Bill Osgerby, from Roger Sabin, ed., *Punk Rock: So What?* 1999.

Punk Rock influences of the New York scene, the irony, pessimism, and amateur style of the music took on overt social and political implications, and British Punk became as self-consciously proletarian as it was aesthetic.

It is true that unemployment and poor social conditions provoke angry feelings of alienation and frustration. It is also true that these feelings can be expressed in many ways. Crime has been the most popular response in recent times, but at this place and time the hoodlums began playing guitars instead of committing petty crimes of frustration. "To ignore the obvious connections between the Punk phenomenon and economic and social inequalities in Great Britain would be to deny the validity of the philosophical underpinnings of the movement. Punk in Britain was essentially a movement consisting of underprivileged working-class white youths. Many of them felt their social situation deeply and used the medium of Punk to express their dissatisfaction."

The purpose of saying this is to give a basis for where the Punks are coming from and why they hold the ideas they do. It would be a lie, however, to say that these original Punks had well-developed social and political theories. They were against all the standard -isms, but were more apt to spit and swear than to explain their feelings to the mainstream public. "These were Punks, not social activists, and their message was bleak. The Sex Pistols' music was an outburst of hatred and despair. Face life as we see it, they cried—frustrating, meaningless, and ugly. Scream it out with us . . . 'There's no future!'"

The Political Goals of Punk Rock

The goal of these original Punks was to express their rage in a harsh and original way. The most hated thing in the world was someone who was a conformist. Many Punk bands have built their platforms or messages with the advocacy and admittance of nonconformity. Conformity is rejected on every front possible in order to seek the truth or sometimes merely to shock people. What is so wrong with conformity? The noted sociologist Elliot Aronson defines conformity as the following: "a change in a person's behavior or opinions as a result of real or imagined pressure from a person or group of people." The real or imagined pressure that Punks reject is not only the physical kind or the interest to be accepted, but the kind of conformity "that results from the observation of others for the purpose of gaining information about proper behavior. . . ."

Punks question conformity not only by looking and sounding different (which has debatable importance), but by questioning the prevailing modes of thought. Questions about things that others take for granted related to work, race, sex, and our own selves are not asked by the conformist whose ideas are determined by those around her. The nonconformist does not rely on others to determine her own reality.

The questioning of conformity involves the questioning of authority as well. Punks do not have a great deal of respect for authority of any kind. . . . In general, authority has been looked at as a great evil-causing agent. From the German Nazis in World War Two, to the subjects of Stanley Milgram's shock experiments, to today's police force, it has been proven that unjustified obedience to authority has resulted in mass acceptance of harmful actions.

By acting as anti-authoritarian nonconformists, Punks are not usually treated very well by those people whose commands to conform are rejected. Society has used language to create a negative image of those who pursue nonconformist means. "For 'individualist' or 'nonconformist,' we can substitute 'deviant;' for 'conformist' we can substitute 'team player.'" This is exactly what modern society has done.

We have seen that nonconformists "may be praised by historians or idolized in films or literature long after the fact" of their nonconformity. As for their own time, the nonconformist is labeled a rebel, a deviant, or a troublemaker by the status quo she is going against. Corporate music and fashion magazines that banned or ridiculed Punk for the last twenty years now hail many bands as 'ground breakers' or talented originators. Corporate music executives once disgusted by Punk are now signing young bands left and right in an effort to make money off the 'cutting edge,' nonconformist sounds.

While mass acceptance may be tempting and even lucrative for some, this quote by Dick Lucas of the English bands Subhumans and Citizen Fish sums up the feelings many Punks have towards society and mainstream culture:

I have never come to terms with the idea that I am 'part of society' and should construct my actions to suit the prevailing moods of conformity, acceptance and achievement. Closed by the rigorous mind training of school and media, the mass mentality of Western culture revolves around upholding the past to attempt to secure the future, whilst suffering the present as beyond its control, 'safe' in the hands of government who feed the present to the masses as a product of technological/material/industrial progress.

CHAPTER

EXAMINING POP CULTURE

The Dangers of Rock and Roll

Early Fears About Rock Music

Trent Hill

Parents and other authority figures found several reasons to fear rock and roll in its early years. These op-
ponents to rock music believed that the beat and
lyrics encouraged premarital and extramarital intercourse; censorship of "off-color" songs became commonplace. Trent Hill asserts that many white middle-
class Americans were threatened by the influence of
African American music on white musicians and teenagers and also believed that rock and roll concerts encouraged teen violence. Hill is a musician and former
professor of English at Clemson University in Clemson, South Carolina.

ROCK & ROLL MUSIC ESTABLISHED SOCIAL CON-
texts in which subterranean social forces could assert themselves, find an outlet for expression, and resolve their various
antagonisms (or, perhaps, reinforce these antagonisms). Just as
all of these forces were not "progressive," neither were all of
these resolutions. But that is not what is at issue in the movements to contain rock & roll; the issue is that these various
contending tendencies were given a voice, that they came into
the open, established connections, and found reinforcement
for their sense and practice of applied (if unreflective) antino-
mianism: rock & roll seemed to call for a realignment of energies at both the psychic and social levels. While that may have
been fine for the kids, for their parents and the other authorities rock & roll was a threatening reminder of the existence of

■

Excerpted from "The Enemy Within: Censorship in Rock Music in the 1950s," by
Trent Hill, *South Atlantic Quarterly*, vol. 90, no. 4 (Fall 1991). Copyright © 1991,
Duke University Press. All rights reserved. Reprinted with permission.

others and otherness that set a dangerous precedent that had to be examined, understood, criticized, and controlled. Gertrude Samuels, writing for the *New York Times Magazine*, stated what was the critical question that parents, congressmen, preachers, and other wielders of power and authority deliberated, at times obsessively, throughout the mid-to-late 1950s: "What is it that makes teen-agers . . . throw off their inhibitions as though at a revivalist meeting?" The answer to this question—and the implications drawn from it—took many forms:

A Sexualized Beat

(1) *The Beat.* Both its admirers and detractors agreed that one characteristic defined rock & roll as a musical genre (even if they disagreed as to whether or not it was truly music): its beat. It was the beat—repetitive, powerful, and pulsating—that both energized the kids and enraged the censorial Mammadaddy. Alan Freed's understanding of the beat was relatively historical and complex: "It began on the levees and plantations, took in folk songs, and features blues and rhythm. It's the rhythm that gets the kids. They are starved for music they can dance to after all those years of crooners." The music was always described in terms of its beat; the only question was whether this beat bore with it a positive or negative ideological valence. Not all the authorities shared Freed's optimism. According to one "expert," the dancing inspired by rock & roll was "primitive," of a sort that "demonstrated the violent mayhem long repressed everywhere on earth"; in conclusion, he warned that if "we cannot stem the tide with its waves of rhythmic narcosis and of future waves of vicarious craze, we are preparing our own downfall in the midst of pandemic funeral dances." If this piece of Cold War era "expertise" strikes us as a finely wrought bit of hysteria, we should note that this hysteria in the face of the beat, along with the confused network of middle-class anxieties that made it seem like a sensible reaction, was quite widespread among critics of rock & roll, and indeed has continued as a theme in criticism right up to the present day. According to Allan Bloom, rock & roll is indeed no more and no less than the savage and primitive rhythm of darkest Africa; furthermore, "[y]oung people know that rock has the beat of sexual intercourse."

Much of the fear associated with rock & roll did in fact derive from its mimetic affinities to sex, and the associated fears that it (and the culture that surrounded it) encouraged and legitimated sex outside of marriage. Yet there were other anxieties that attended to the beat. It worked to consolidate large, amorphous gatherings of youth (as well as the even larger, amorphous culture of youth), providing 1950s teenagers with a cultural focus that encompassed wide areas of appearance, attitude, and behavior. Some observers thought that this power of the music proved that it was a new form of mind control with dangerous affinities to fascism. Herbert von Karijian, the conductor of the Berlin Philharmonic, was precisely vague when he summarized all of these anxieties in his attempt at "explaining" rock & roll: "Strange things happen in the blood stream when a musical resonance coincides with the beat of the human pulse."

Even within the music business, there was much anxiety about the new music (which was really not so new after all). In an influential unsigned article in its 23 February 1955 issue, the editors of *Variety* magazine issued "A Warning to the Music Business." The occasion for this warning was the sudden popularity of r&b songs, such as "Sixty-Minute Man" and "Work with Me, Annie," whose rhythms underscored the scantily clad sexual message of the lyrics—or, as the editors described them, "leer-ics":

> What are we talking about? We're talking about "rock & roll," about "hug," and "squeeze," and kindred euphemisms which are attempting a total breakdown of all reticence about sex.

The record labels most widely associated with the dissemination of these "blue notes" were the smaller labels, such as King and Imperial, that were "heedless" of responsibility, as might have been expected, since they did not operate within the social and ideological boundaries of respectability as defined by the legitimate major labels. But major labels were guilty of the same sins as the independent operators, and were, due to the greater degree of trust and responsibility invested in them as known quantities, even "guiltier" in a large social sense.

The effect of the *Variety* editorial (and a similar one that ran in *Billboard* magazine) was immediate and striking, at least at the level of the grand sociopolitical gesture. Some newspapers reprinted parts of it and added their voices to the call for cleanliness on the nation's airwaves. Record labels disavowed that they ever intentionally released discs that contained double entendres, and fell all over themselves endorsing *Variety's* position. The Boston Catholic Youth Organization began to police record hops (which were suspected of providing fronts for illicit sexual behavior) and monitor radio stations more closely. And, while Boston has traditionally been the site of the most extreme episodes of censorship (going back to the banning of John Cleland's *Memoirs)*, stations all across the country announced that they would no longer program "off-color" records.

Fear of African-American Culture

(2) *Jungle Strains.* These records were "off-color" in both the moral and the racial sense; while sexually frank lyrics had long been accepted in r&b songs, it was only when these records became objects of consumption for white kids that anybody (least of all *Variety* magazine) had any kind of problem with them. According to the February 1955 piece in *Variety*, music of the past contained the same kinds of coded reference to matters sexual; the "only difference is that this sort of lyric then was off in a corner by itself. It was the music underworld—not the mainstream." Its success, that is, established its guilt, identified it as a threat, and demonstrated the necessity of controlling it. This new outbreak of cultural miscegenation could only spell trouble for white America, which lived in a guilty fear of African-Americans and their culture. Guilty, because of the growing consensus that racism and segregation were evils that had to be remedied; fear, because this culture of poverty was ambiguously coded as a source of both liberation and delinquency. It (and its musical expressions) stood for what was, in McCarthyite America, coded as "primitive." Beyond the reach of modern society, deemed too unimportant to warrant direct surveillance by those in positions of power and responsibility, African-American culture seemed to be a repository where sexuality, supposedly untouched by social convention and bourgeois ethics that allowed it to function only within mar-

riage and property relations, flourished unfettered. White intellectuals found this repository irresistible. According to Norman Mailer,

> . . . the Negro had stayed alive and begun to grow by following the need of his body where he could. . . . [T]he Negro . . . could rarely afford the sophisticated inhibitions of civilization, and so he kept for his survival the art of the primitive, he lived in the enormous present, he subsisted for his Saturday night kicks, relinquishing the pleasures of the mind for the more obligatory pleasures of the body, and in his music he gave voice to the character and quality of his existence.

And of course this valorization of the Negro as culturally independent comes through to some degree in Alan Freed's defense of rock & roll. The music that "began on the levees and plantations" was to be the means by which teenagers could be restored to their bodies in the vehicle of the dance.

Not everybody in white, middle-class America—the ruling class that supplied society with its ruling ideas—took very kindly to this democratic and market-driven Negrification of its youth. One of its responses was only somewhat more subtle than it was doomed: record companies, concerned with the economic and ideological viability of marketing yowling black folk to white kids, originally sought to allay their fears and the fears of parents by having "safe" white songsters produce dessicated cover versions of the real Negro thing. But these ersatz productions were not successful for long: Pat Boone was not Little Richard, and despite all apparent similarities, the song they sang was not the same, even if the title of both of their records was "Tutti Frutti," their chord progressions the same, and their lyrics identical. In addition, overt racism was at least occasionally an important component in white American power's reaction. Some whites felt that the goal of the Negro was to overrun the white race by a long campaign of miscegenation. According to Edwin White, a member of the Mississippi House, "the normal and inevitable result through the years will be intermarriage and a mix-breed population."

Some white southerners felt that rock & roll music was a part of this campaign, and traced the music's popularity to part of a fiendish plot by the NAACP to "infiltrate" southern white teenagers. In Birmingham, Alabama, the local White Citizen's Council petitioned juke box owners to remove the "immoral" records, which were "the basic, heavy-beat music of Negroes [that] appeals to the base in man, brings out animalism and vulgarity." The author of that description, Asa Carter, was an authority on the music based on his having "swung a few niggers [him]self." As might have been expected from such an organization, the White Citizen's Council immediately put their theory into practice; the day after this proclamation, a few of its members rushed the stage at a whites-only Nat King Cole concert, assaulting the singer and injuring him slightly before they were dragged off the stage.

This episode suggests something that is, so far as I know, unique to rock & roll among forms of pop culture: it has throughout its career been identified with social movements and tendencies that represent the boundaries of the permissibly progressive (which is what the civil rights movement was in the 1950s). It is perhaps this political affiliation that the music has maintained up until the present, and what has spared it from the severe and overt repression that some other pop culture forms (such as movies and comic books) have faced during the same time period. Indeed, all of the rock and rock-related records that have been brought to trial for or accused of obscenity in the 1980s—from the Dead Kennedy's *In God We Trust, Inc.*, to N.W.A.'s *AmeriKKKa's Most Wanted*, to 2 Live Crew's *As Nasty as They Wanna Be*—have been defended and acquitted on grounds that they are political discourses and are protected as such under current law.

If rock & roll was identified with the expansion of rights for African-Americans during the 1950s, we must not overlook the fact that this identification was not unambiguously positive, even in the more liberal sectors of the society. The history of exclusion that Mailer draws on is one rich in consequences: if the Negro is a repository of drives excised from white America by means of the methodical application of paranoia, the Negro has been freed from this fate by an economic and social exclusion that has made him a victim of poverty and a candidate for delinquency. Most of the positive, liberating characteristics that Mailer uses to define his white/black hipster are, after all, characteristics that would mark a white teenager as a delinquent. And African-Americans were always regarded in the 1950s as a group "at risk" for delinquency; it was their schools that had the most problems with student discipline, their neighborhoods that had the most problems with gangs, their insertion into former white enclaves that gave rise to social unrest. Just as their culture was a resource for liberation, their very existence was a catalyst for social upheavals and racial tensions.

Encouraging Violence

(3) *Rock & Riot.* If the release of the presocial (or at least pre-McCarthy), primitive, and negroid id was an indirect affinity that rock & roll had with juvenile delinquency, white America worried even more about what seemed to be direct and blatant connections between rock & roll and teenage savagery. . . .

For starters, the culture of rock & roll consisted of a rich iconography of delinquency. The styles we associate with it—leather jackets, blue jeans, the "ducktail" haircut, the preference for the motorcycle—were all associated in the consciousness of the 1950s with rebellious, discontented, working-class teenagers who were always "at risk" for delinquency. In the words of some in attendance at the National Association of Secondary School Principals: "You can't put a kid into a monkey suit like one of these blue jeans outfits and expect him to make any kind of good record for himself." These associations were solidified by such movies as *The Wild One* and *Rebel without a Cause*, which suggested to parents and other emissaries of power that this manifestation of working-class youth culture denied the validity of those long-term life projects—the "American Dream"—that so many of the other battles of the period tried to affirm. Rock & roll culture was a culture of the immediate, of physical pleasures affirmed as ends-in-themselves, all of which evoked a dangerous denial of interest in long-term consequences and responsibilities, and a death of ambition that could only be an ominous sign in a scruffy prole teenager. And it was even more worrisome that rock & roll offered a system of objects and roles that were both attractive and accessible to middle-class youth.

The nascence of rock & roll indeed appeared to offer not only a theory and iconography of delinquency and teenage rebellion, but its practice and fruition as well. The early accounts of the new music in newspapers and journals are all descriptions of a struggle, if not a riot. According to the *New York Times* account of one Freed show in New York, thousands upon thousands of teenagers lined up on Washington's Birthday (a school holiday) for hours to see the show, in the process smashing windows, crashing barricades, and destroying the ticket seller's box at the theater where the show was held. All of this was the doing, according to the headline, of the "blue-jean and leather-jacket set," a headline that supplied for the parents the sartorial codes that defined the meaning of the music. (In case the connection wasn't obvious enough, the story ran on a page alongside stories of slain young robbers, exhortations to establish dress codes, and a host of denunciations of the music.)

Indeed, in the mainstream press of the day, all signs indicated that rock & roll and violence were directly and irredeemably linked. One rock & roll riot at Fort Bragg was cut short with tear gas; in Cambridge, a rock & roll fundraising event at the Massachusetts Institute of Technology (MIT) turned into a fracas after it became evident that there would be no dancing allowed. The culprits were "these kids . . . that you knew weren't from any college." Riots in Asbury Park, San Jose, Dallas, and Boston destroyed property and sent some people to the hospital; and after the riot in Boston (which, as Linda Martin and Kerry Segrave argue, was as likely a police riot as anything else), Alan Freed was indicted for "inciting the unlawful destruction of property." Apparently, after a night of exceptionally tight crowd control by the police, the teenage audience at Freed's show in Boston got out of their seats and rushed into the aisles to dance, at which point the head of security ordered the lights turned on. Freed allegedly told the audience: "I guess the police here in Boston don't want you kids to have a good time," which set off a riot. Worse, people were mugged, robbed, and stabbed outside the arena (which was in a high-crime area) before, during, and after the show, which for many confirmed the connection between crime, violence, and rock & roll.

The Class Conflicts of Rock Concerts

But the problems with violence at rock & roll shows were not so much attributable to the music as to the fact that these shows were large gatherings at which a whole host of class conflicts played themselves out. Early rock & roll shows were interracial affairs; African-Americans made up between one- and two-thirds of the audience, which also contained white working-class kids who found the more "hillbilly" aspect of the music appealing. This was a highly volatile concatenation of class and race antagonisms that neither the music nor the police could easily contain, and the sexually charged atmosphere of these shows and record hops provided the spark that could set off conflagrations at almost any time. We could argue that, just as these shows provided arenas in which repressed hostilities could return to the psychosocial surface, the incidence of these explosions provided rare occasions in which hostilities could be discussed, albeit in a highly mediated fashion. Moreover, it should not surprise us that the music was held accountable for these explosions of hostility.

They were symptoms of a disease that was too shameful, too fraught with consequences, to be discussed in the light of day, and as a result the only therapy allowed was to make the symptoms disappear.

The Vulgar Values of Rock

Stuart Goldman

Writing in 1989, Stuart Goldman decries the hedo-
nistic values of rock music in the following viewpoint.
He contends that rock musicians glorify homosexuality and sadomasochism and are insincere in their support for social issues. Despite their alleged love for
freedom, he writes, rock musicians are quick to attack
those who oppose their own values. Goldman also argues that rock and roll is selfish and anarchic. He
concludes that rock music is "junk food" that destroys
the soul. Goldman is a former music critic for the *Los
Angeles Times*. He is also an investigative reporter and
a writer whose works have appeared in the *National
Review* and other publications.

WHAT ARE THE VALUES THAT ROCK PURVEYS?
Back in 1966 Bob Dylan told an interviewer, "if people knew
what this stuff was about, we'd probably all get arrested." The
words rock 'n' roll—in the original patois drawn from the lingo
of the blues and jazz players of the early Fifties—were synony-
mous with the sex act. But in the days of Elvis and Jerry Lee,
there was a certain understated quality about the sexual content
in rock. And it was plain, old-fashioned heterosexual sex, generally "love," that was hinted at both in the twitching pelvis of
Elvis and in the boy-next-door appeal of Ricky Nelson. Not so
today. Sex is the main ingredient in rock music, and the artists
and producers who crank it out make no bones about this. And
we're talking about sex of every possible variety.

■

Sexual Perversity in Rock Music

Not only is the music scene [in the late 1980s] rife with homosexual rock groups, like Frankie Goes to Hollywood, that hawk their lifestyle in their music, but the cleverer rock stars (David Bowie, Michael Jackson, Mick Jagger) maintain a calculated androgyny so as to appeal equally to both the boys and the girls. Likewise, female rockers like the lankjawed Michelle Shocked, the bald-pated Sinead O'Connor, and the muscular Tracy Chapman have opted for the androgynous look. And we musn't forget Boy George—the first drag queen ever to achieve superstar status.

This heavy sexuality is not just a matter of atmosphere. Rock has become distinguishable from overt pornography mainly in degree. Snicker if you like, but a brief look at MTV will bear this out. Almost all of Prince's videos feature the half-pint superstar cavorting with a bevy of scantily clad women. Likewise the stubble-faced hunk, George Michael. Female rocker Lita Ford, hanging out of her low-cut T-shirt, gropes her guitar for all it's worth in her videos. Perhaps the most blatant (and surely the dumbest) sex video on the tube is "Let's Put the X in the Sex" (just like a muscle and it makes me wanna flex), by the over-the-hill glam-rock band Kiss.

But it is music selling itself under the moniker of heavy metal, performed by groups like Slayer, Coven, the Damned, and Cycle Sluts from Hell, in which sex appears in its most blatant and perverse forms. Primarily pushing sadomasochistic sex heavy metal does not neglect occultism, suicide, and murder. You needn't go to a slasher film to see a woman being disemboweled in a satanic ritual—just turn on your local music video station. In short, rock has trivialized evil. Thus, songs like Slayer's "Spill the Blood" and "Mandatory Suicide," or The Misfit's "Can I Go Out and Kill Tonight?" are treated as silly or cute by the rock critics.

This would be still more depressing if there weren't a comedic element here. Just imagine a group of dour-faced politicians sitting around discussing the validity of lyrics like "Bend over and smell my anal vapor / Your face is my toilet paper." (For these lyrics were indeed read into the Congressional Record during the 1985 Senate hearings on rock lyrics.)

It is not only the lyrics, however, that carry a strong message of sexual perversity. The stock costume worn by heavy-metal groups features torn T-shirt (or no shirt), leather pants with an ostentatious codpiece, boots, and an assortment of studs, chains, earrings, and other jewelry. Certain onstage antics are also de rigueur. The rocker must leer, grimace, sweat profusely, leap about like a spastic, and emphasize his guitar's phallic potential for all it's worth. Meanwhile, the kids in the audience react on cue: they bash each other, flail about, crush themselves into a painful mass, thrust clenched fists in the air—in addition to your traditional displays of screaming, crying, and fainting familiar from the Rolling Stones fan club in the 1960s (average age: 11).

Glorifying Depravity

"Rock music is the quintessence of vulgarity. It's crude, loud, and tasteless," wrote Robert Pattison in *The Triumph of Vulgarity*. But this vulgarity has a serious purpose: the undermining of traditional values. In order to obscure this fact, of which they themselves may be only dimly aware, rock stars have learned from their brethren in the film industry the value of entertainment doublespeak. Thus, after he was criticized for his highly explicit video of "I Want Your Sex," George Michael dutifully explained that the song was about "monogamous sex" (rock's idea of chastity).

Similarly, to show its concern for suffering humanity, *Spin* magazine (which emits constant attacks on traditional Judeo-Christian values) features in each issue an AIDS column, which is not exactly up to *New England Journal of Medicine* standards. The November [1988] column, for example, tried to dissuade its readers from believing the "propaganda" that AIDS is a virus; rather, according to *Spin*'s experts, AIDS is a form of syphilis that can be easily cured by a simple injection of typhoid vaccine. The November *Spin* also had a first: a condom inserted between the pages of each copy. According to publisher Bob Guccione Jr. (right—his son), the condom [is] "a statement . . . an attempt to do something about safe sex."

Indeed, rock as a whole has mastered the art of turning depravity into good PR. Witness the numerous rock stars who have jumped onto the RAD (Rockers against Drugs) bandwagon. The basic schtick is simple: become an addict; then, after years of abuse, come clean (or at least say you've come clean—who checks, anyway?) in a heartfelt public statement. If this proves impossible, paying homage to a former bandmate who has died of a drug overdose will do in a pinch.

You might therefore be surprised to find that rock has its own code of ethics. In rock mythology, we are all brethren—one people—spiritually united with the cosmos. Punk, hard rock, minimalist rock, art rock—it matters not: this belief lies at the core of each of them. However, the rocker feels that we are kept from this—our "natural" state of oneness with the Universe—by "them": the government, teachers, politicians, our parents. All the usual suspects. "We Are the World," whose lyrics were written by Michael Jackson, was the most direct testimony to the pantheist-globalist basis of rock.

In celebrating this formless pantheist ideal, rockers follow in the great liberal tradition of grandstanding their humanitarian ideals. Let's see . . . we've had the Concert for Bangladesh, Live Aid, Band-Aid, Farm Aid, Hands across America, Human Rights Now!—not to mention innumerable benefits for AIDS

Rock and Its Romantic Worship of Death

Rock and Romanticism share an aesthetic appreciation of death as the ultimate form of excess, a notion perfectly realized in Edward Onslow Ford's memorial to Shelley in University College, Oxford. The drowned Percy Bysshe Shelley's limbs glisten in Carrara marble. He is dazzling in death, and the sculpture, in emphasizing his lolling penis and languishing posture, suggests that death is the acme of postcoital abandon. Ford's monument anticipates the full-blown vulgarity of popular Romanticism, whose dead heroes Jimi Hendrix or Janis Joplin are similarly revered for having climaxed to eternity.

The rock hero most beautiful in death is Jim Morrison, who died in his bathtub in Paris. In legend, he died of

(though no AIDS-Aid) and—oh, yes—Nelson Mandela's Seventieth Birthday. How much money or food actually gets through to the celebrated victim? Who knows—or, apart from Bob Geldof, cares? What is clear is that the events themselves present tremendous opportunities for publicity. And we've yet to see multi-millionaires of the Springsteen/Sting ilk donating any significant percentage of their yearly incomes to the causes that are so beloved by them. Until that happens, I'm inclined to agree with Allan Bloom, who, in *The Closing of the American Mind*, writes off rock's humanitarian efforts as "a smarmy, hypocritical version of brotherly love."

Indeed, the true god of the rock belief system is the self, transmogrified into some vast collective cosmos. Rock pantheism is Me writ large.

The Theology and Politics of Rock

Once rock is viewed as a New Age system of thought and ethics, we are not surprised to find it anti-rational and obsessed with the present moment. In Bloom's words, "When the pantheist equates self and God, he demotes thought to a

an overdose (the cause of his death has never been formally established) and was buried without autopsy or proper identification—facts which have fed the Romantic myth that self-annihilation is perfect self-realization. The fans of the Lizard King still believe he is alive somewhere, like King Arthur. Morrison dead in his tub is the vulgar duplicate of David's "Marat," cut off in mid-sentence, arrested forever in a revolutionary youth, powerful in martyrdom, though Morrison's is a self-inflicted martyrdom. . . .

The pantheist, face forward toward infinity, views death as the mysterious catalyst of the transformations that lead from one state to another. Rock's young martyrs command allegiance in death as vulgar embodiments of the Romantic energy that challenges time to make us all in all.

Robert Pattison, *The Triumph of Vulgarity: Rock Music in the Mirror of Romanticism*, 1987.

secondary role in the universe and elevates feeling as the fundamental way of knowing. . . . he does away with history and inaugurates a perpetual now. Rock follows this tradition. It is not only not reasonable, it is hostile to reason." Rock stands essentially for the liberation of emotion from the tyranny of reason. It is a revolutionary proclamation from the Id.

The politics of rock derive naturally from this theology. It is hopeless to expect any support for an ordered society from a set of emotional responses to the latest stimuli. Being a conservative and a rocker, for instance, is not really possible. (I concede that quite a number of conservatives act as though this were not the case.) Conservatism—a doctrine of balance, moderation, and restraints upon appetite (a "manly, regulated liberty" in Burke's phrase)—is and must be anathema to rock.

Marxism—also, in its way, a doctrine of order—has a more ambiguous attitude to rock. Sixties Marxists in the West were, of course, rockers all. They loved—still do love—to profess belief in the classless society. It sometimes seemed that Che Guevara had a string of hits rather than a string of revolutions to his credit. But Marxists in Marxist countries are fiercely hostile to rock, regarding it as a form of ideological poison. The contradiction is easily resolved, comrade, if we see rock as a disintegrative factor, undermining authority, spreading harmful practices and dividing families and generations.

Also, as Bloom says, "the Left has given rock music a free ride. Abstracting it from the capitalist element in which it flourishes, they regard it as the people's art, coming from beneath the bourgeoisie's layers of cultural repression." This is of course an illusion. Rock is created by writers and musicians who are largely middle-class in their origins and bourgeois in their view of money (if not in their lifestyles), and promoted by capitalist methods in a capitalist economy. The stance of rock may be anti-bourgeois, but as Eugene Ionesco points out, "All bourgeois are detestable, but the most detestable kind of bourgeois is the anti-bourgeois kind of bourgeois."

Is rock, then, "liberal"? Liberalism, it is fair to say, is helpless before any assault by rock on conventional moral standards. Hooked on an extremist interpretation of the First Amendment and on a wholly subjectivist notion of taste, liberals simply have no basis for resisting the wilder excesses of heavy metal. Equally, however, the liberal stress on "sensitivity" to the feelings of others, notably other groups, is often uncomfortable with the crude, hostile, and vicious elements in rock. Liberals prefer *Masterpiece Theatre*. Nor can feminists wholly approve the sexism in rock. . . .

So if rock is neither conservative nor Marxist nor liberal, that leaves the anti-authority doctrine of anarchism. This is nearer to the mark; rockers routinely denounce "the system"—governments, parents, teachers, etc. However, they usually do this while driving around in limos, talking on car phones with managers, lawyers, and accountants. Ask any young rocker his dream and you'll find that it involves wealth, fame, and power.

Attacks on Conservatism

Rock politics, in short, is a sort of parasitic anarchism. Rockers are comfortably aware that the hated system will doubtless outlive them, continuing to provide its despised benefits. At the heavy-metal extreme, this becomes a form of hypocritical nihilism in which all the normal values of civilized decency are sneered at and—in everyday business transactions—relied upon.

Thus, while rock professes a love of freedom, it is quick to attack any belief system that opposes it. The two most powerful rock magazines, *Rolling Stone* and *Spin*, consistently feature articles hostile to conservative thought. In a *Spin* article entitled "Music under Siege," Adam Greenfield whined for 1,500 words about a bill (introduced by the "notorious reactionary" Senator Strom Thurmond) that would punish producers of child pornography and other pedophile-oriented material. Greenfield calls the bill (which might well affect certain record producers) "a beachhead for right-wing brownshirts and geeks" and warns that it not only would have disastrous effects on groups like Screaming Cocks and Scraping Fetus Off the Wheel, but would "virtually deplete the entire content of modern culture." (That's how rock intellectuals talk.)

Most conservatives who work in the business (and there are some) remain in the closet. Mark Frejulian, manager of a stable of popular rock groups, puts it bluntly: "If you're in the business and you openly espouse right-wing ideals, you're out. If you're a conservative, you learn to keep your mouth shut."

Frejulian related an incident in which a group wanted to inject a moral message into a particular song. The record-company exec blew up. "Listen," he seethed, "the fans want sex, drugs, and rock 'n' roll. If you're not prepared to give it to them, you might as well get the hell out of the business."

Former *Chappell Music* staff writer Eric Apoe openly admits his conservative beliefs. "This business's idea of ethics is having an AIDS benefit and singing songs like 'I Want Your Sex,'" Apoe scoffs. "It's absurd!" Though he agrees that the business can be tough on you if you're openly conservative, Apoe says he feels a moral responsibility to the audience. "I'm not going to be coerced into writing porn-rock," he states flatly. "I need to be able to look at myself in the mirror every day."

But rock has learned how to immunize itself from criticism by employing the standard liberal methodology. The moment you call rock's ethics into question, you are branded an enemy of "freedom of expression." Put rock down and you're "anti-art." At worst you're simply labeled "uncool." When Tipper Gore's group tried to get labels affixed to LPs simply warning buyers of the sexual content of lyrics, the rock world—led by Frank Zappa—howled en masse. All the usual labels—"fascists," "book burners," "Nazis"—were flung about. No one ever mentioned the aggressive tactics of the rockers themselves.

The Death of Rock

Rock music is junk food for the soul—a diet of sex, drugs, and non-stop pleasure-seeking which all too often is a deadly poison. I am not speaking figuratively, as witness the list of dead rock stars. Two of them—Jimi Hendrix and Jim Morrison—choked on their own vomit while in the throes of drug overdose. The King, Elvis Presley—his 280-pound body polluted by the drugs he had lived on—was found dead at the foot of his toilet bowl, his pajama bottoms around his ankles. One would be hard-pressed to call that a graceful exit.

Of course, dead rockers fit nicely into rock's philosophy. Courageous men and women who died in the full flight of creativity . . . shining stars who burned brightly, if only for a moment. Alas, the truth is less appealing. Rockers live in search of the impossible: an ever-fleeting pleasure that's always just out of reach, illusions of a perpetual youth that fades away, adoration from a fickle public that inevitably casts them aside in favor of a newer model. In the end, rock proves to be a cruel mistress.

"Rock 'n' roll will never die!" the rocker boasts, thrusting a clenched fist into the air. But the truth is, rock 'n' roll is already dead. It died in 1977 with its first god, Elvis Presley. What exists today is something else—a cheap imitation of the original model. In place of the musical vitality that inspired the pioneers, there is now merely the debased desire to shock and titillate. George Orwell, in his essay on Salvador Dali, "Benefit of Clergy," described the process whereby an artist solves the problem of his meager or failing talent. In doing so, he described the recent history of rock:

> There is always one escape: into wickedness. Always do the thing that will shock and wound people . . . throw a little boy off a bridge, strike an old doctor across the face with a whip and break his spectacles—or, at any rate, dream about doing such things . . . gouge the eyes out of dead donkeys with a pair of scissors. Along those lines you can always feel yourself original. And after all, it pays! . . . You could even top it all up with religious conversion, moving at one hop and without of repentance from the fashionable salons of Paris to Abraham's bosom.

Nonetheless, rock's ranks continue to swell. It continues to breed new addicts. And why not? Look at what it promises: eternal youth, bliss, happiness, fulfillment for a terminally empty soul. And of course these are lies—but they're lies that man has been buying ever since Eve took the serpent at his word.

Drug Use by Rock Musicians

Richard Harrington

In the following selection, Washington Post staff writer Richard Harrington examines the longstanding connection between drug use and rock and roll. Drugs such as marijuana and LSD have been positively portrayed in rock music, he notes, but musicians have also used rock to warn against the dangers of heroin. He writes that although most musicians are aware of the dangers of drug abuse, many mistakenly believe that drug use improves their skills. Harrington also suggests that rock musicians and their teenage fans use dangerous drugs such as heroin as a way to rebel against society.

WHAT IS IT ABOUT HEROIN AND MUSICIANS? Though songwriters almost never portray this drug positively, it seems never to be far from the musical world. And when Smashing Pumpkins keyboard player Jonathan Melvoin died of an overdose on July 12, 1996, it was only the latest renewal of an odd, cyclical affair.

Substance abuse is a problem throughout American society, with heroin unquestionably on the rise: The National Institute on Drug Abuse estimates there are as many as 1 million heroin addicts in the United States, and another 3 million users. Perhaps it is unfair that the focus has again fallen on entertainers.

Still, the history of heroin and popular music goes back almost 50 years, through three waves of strobe-lit celebrity failures. It's a strange, unnerving story.

■

From Richard Harrington, "The Heroin Experience: The Drug Has Smacked into More than One Generation of Musicians," *The Washington Post*, August 11, 1996.

Music and heroin first came together in a big way in the late '40s. That's when heroin and alcohol almost destroyed jazz's be-bop revolution by crushing the life of its spark plug, Charlie Parker, and putting many of its leaders in prison or in graves. The second time around for heroin and music came about two decades later when the drug claimed some of rock's major figures. Now, once again, it has come home to thin the ranks in the rock community, with Seattle, the birthplace of grunge, hit particularly hard.

Other drugs have a different link with music. Marijuana and LSD have been and continue to be positively portrayed in lyrics. Cocaine seems to provoke as many pro-coke songs as anti-. But music about heroin has never been positive. For instance, a 1972 study of drug songs made in the wake of the Jimi Hendrix-Janis Joplin-Jim Morrison tragedies found 67 that were anti-heroin and none that were pro-heroin. That didn't stop critics from finding references to the drug in such unlikely songs as the Beatles' "Hey Jude" (in the line "let her into your heart") and Simon and Garfunkel's "Bridge Over Troubled Water" (in which "If you need a friend/ I am sailing right behind" allegedly described an on-call pusher).

The most obvious heroin song, the Velvet Underground's "Heroin," is surprisingly elusive, despite such lines as "Heroin will be the death of me/ But it's my wife and it's my life . . . because a mainer in my vein/ Leads to the center of my brain/ And then I'm better off dead . . . I'm gonna try to nullify my life." The song's creator, Lou Reed, has always insisted "Heroin" is neither pro nor con, but simply descriptive. The song clearly recognizes heroin's seductive appeal—not only in its lyrics but in its musical pacing—but it also provides an unflinching portrait of its consequences, as does Neil Young's "The Needle and the Damage Done." Provoked by the 1972 death of Crazy Horse guitarist Danny Whitten, it remains one of the most virulent anti-drug songs of all time, despite its tone of sympathy ("I've seen the needle and the damage done/ A little part of it in everyone/ But every junkie's like a setting sun").

On the 1992 Alice in Chains album, "Dirt," singer and chief songwriter Layne Staley painted a harrowing self-portrait of addiction in such autobiographical confessionals as "Sick Man," "Godsmack" and "Junkhead." Some critics felt

Staley was too ambivalent in his writing, not judgmental enough, but the album as a whole simply addresses what Staley was going through. There have been a number of songs that could be interpreted as tributes—from the little-known Spacemen Three and the overexposed Guns N' Roses ("Mr. Brownstone"), as well as from drug-addled proto-Britbeat bands such as Suede ("Chasing the Dragon").

The newest heroin-related song on the market is more typical: In "Book of Shadows," guitarist Zakk Wylde writes from the point of view of a child watching his father dying from a drug overdose. Inspired by the overdose death [in October 1995] of Wylde's friend Shannon Hoon, the Blind Melon singer, it's called "Throwin' It All Away."

Still, it's guitarist Johnny Thunders who may be the most convoluted embodiment of heroin's consequences. He started out in the New York Dolls, whose drummer, Billy Murcia, died of a Quaalude/alcohol overdose in 1972 and whose second drummer, Jerry Nolan, overdosed on heroin in 1992. Thunders eventually formed the Heartbreakers, whose best known song, "Chinese Rocks," detailed the junkie's debilitating lifestyle. He later did a solo project titled "Too Much Junkie Business," which included an elegy for overdosed Sid Vicious. In the early '80s, the Replacements (a band that eventually imploded because of drugs and alcohol) recorded a Thunders tribute, "Johnny's Gonna Die," which is exactly what Thunders did when he overdosed in 1991.

As an Alanis Morissette hit says: You live, you learn. You die, maybe others learn.

Drugs Do Not Improve Music

Rolling Stones guitarist Keith Richards has long been known for substance abuse, and long-term heroin addiction has physically marked him. His habit was so bad for so many years that Richards's drug supplier, Tony Sanchez, wrote his own memoir, "Up and Down With the Rolling Stones." A few years ago, Richards (now simply a persistent drinker) played down the artistic impact of heroin in an *Option* interview. "You waste yourself too much and too long and then you realize some of the contacts are not quite working. So then you give up."

Aerosmith vocalist Steven Tyler, whose entire band has been

in recovery since bottoming out in 1985, has said much the same thing: "The receptors don't get it anymore. It's like a guy going to a club and the doorman doesn't recognize him anymore."

The reality is that drugs don't improve a musician's technical skills, though some (marijuana, LSD) may alter consciousness and experience. (The Doors, of course, took their name from "Doors of Perception," Aldous Huxley's paean to peyote and mescaline.) Others (speed, cocaine) may affect a musician's endurance, but few artists have credited drugs as creative partners and many, particularly those in recovery, have spoken about the negative impact of drug use on their musicianship, about how ineffective their performances are under the influence.

Some players simply use drugs as a crutch to overcome insecurities (personal and musical) or to numb their pain (real or imagined). Others use them to overcome the boredom of the road or the boredom of being off the road. Richards once noted, "Every minute that I'm off the road I either turn into an alcoholic or a junkie 'cause I've got nothing else to do."

And there are some who use their pop celebrity as an excuse for their behavior or to validate addictions. They are surrounded not only by enablers who cater to their every need and justify substance abuse as part of the overall package, but also by friends and fans all too willing to donate or to share illegal substances to connect with the stars.

Drugs as a Reward

It's worth noting that there's nothing to suggest that musicians or other entertainers are more inclined to abuse drugs than any other group; it's that their transgressions are more easily, and eagerly, noted. The inclination to abuse is usually determined by personality characteristics rather than job descriptions, and it is defined by the user's expectations and cultural and social environments.

Yet while drugs continue to intertwine with the lifestyles of many people, only music has its own (overused) slogan, "sex, drugs and rock-and-roll." Generally, that's an indicator of rock's rewards. Call it an environmental hazard: Historically, pop musicians have come up through the club system, playing in bars where drinking is the prime fiscal driver. While most clubs don't feed bands, almost all of them give musicians an open alcohol tab—an invitation to abuse.

The drug corollary is less obvious, but during the '40s and '50s, seedy jazz club owners were known to pay musicians with drugs (most often heroin). The practice wasn't unknown in country music (in his biography, George Jones recalls being paid by his promoters with drugs) or rock (where Three Dog Night had a similar experience).

The most extreme example of that process remains alto saxophonist Parker, who was using heroin long before he changed the sound of jazz with his be-bop innovations. Unfortunately, countless Parker disciples took to heroin, assuming—or hoping—it would allow them to play at their idol's level. It

Drugs Ruined the Punk Scene

In the following excerpt from Please Kill Me: The Uncensored Oral History of Punk, *writer and former punk singer Mick Farren explains how drug use helped destroy the punk scene, in particular the writer Lester Bangs.*

MICK FARREN: Well, it all broke down, didn't it? It was the eighties. And there was cocaine. Shovels full of cocaine. And ingesting drugs doesn't require a lot of talent, and that's why I think we brought ourselves down to Sid, who, it could be said, was the ultimate product of the entire punk movement. I mean Sid was completely worthless, ha ha ha.

So drugs brought money back and Ronald Reagan was elected president, and you know, shit went on. In fact, that's the sad part: hippies survived Nixon, but punk caved in to Ronald Reagan, know what I'm saying? Punk couldn't actually take a good challenge.

I mean, look at Lester Bangs, the great intellectual of the punk movement, this fucked-up Seventh Day Adventist kid who tacked on to rock & roll but really didn't wanna go the distance. Lester got the madness that he knew, peripheral madness, like the guy who goes to a Chi-

couldn't and they didn't. The irony is that Parker's best performances came on those occasions when he was clean.

Parker himself was ashamed of his addiction and literally begged others not to do as he did, advice lost on the likes of Miles Davis, Sonny Rollins, Red Rodney, Frank Morgan, Chet Baker, Stan Getz, Dexter Gordon, Gene Ammons and Art Pepper (the last three served substantial prison terms for heroin possession). In his last years, even Parker couldn't get regular work (club owners and the majority of musicians having grown equally wary of junkies). Physically and psychologically debilitated, Parker suffered a nervous breakdown, lost the cabaret license allowing him to play in New York, and at-

---

nese restaurant and orders the same meal, because that was the first one he ever had and that will do.

It always pissed me off that the man couldn't do anything outside of this very narrow field of rock & roll writing. He couldn't even write a functional book about Blondie; on the other hand, at some given point, he was a better writer than I am, and I'm a very good writer. I mean, take any given paragraph of Lester Bangs, and it's a piece of fucking brilliant writing, but it's all about the same shit. What I'm saying is that if you don't get a life, that's what happens to you.

I just wondered why Lester didn't sit down and write himself a kind of Jim Thompson novel, because god knows, he was prolific enough—I mean, there's so much Lester on the cutting-room floor. It really started to bother me that he wasn't literally going anywhere, and it seemed like the only thing he could fucking do was die. That's really what struck me about Lester—it seemed like a fucking waste of a brain. Because you sure as shit don't have a lot of fun OD'ing on NyQuil. I mean, there are better things to die from.

Legs McNeil and Gillian McCain, *Please Kill Me: The Uncensored Oral History of Punk*, 1996.

tempted suicide. When Parker died in 1955 at age 34, the coroner doing his autopsy thought he was examining the body of a 65-year-old man.

The Effects of Heroin

The drug that maintains a strangely seductive profile in the entertainment world is [approximately] a hundred years old, a morphine-derived painkiller developed in 1898 by the German pharmaceutical giant Bayer. Highly promising at first—heroin didn't have morphine's side effects of nausea and constipation—the drug turned out to be so highly addictive and replete with its own negative side effects that it was quickly banned in many countries, thus ending its future as a legal drug.

Heroin provides an initially intense rush, followed by a warm euphoric high and cool detachment that can last up to six hours. Some users have described it as crawling back into the womb. But it's also enslaving: As a user's tolerance increases, larger and more frequent dosages are needed to achieve a lesser high; eventually addicts switch to lower doses simply to fight off the severe physical symptoms and psychological despair of withdrawal. It has the highest relapse rate of any drug.

"They can get it out of your blood," Parker said, "but they can't get it out of your mind."

And it's now so much easier to get heroin into your body without going through a vein: It's cheaper and more ubiquitous than ever, and an increase in the purity of powder heroin (from 4 percent in 1980 to as much as 70 percent today) allows users to snort or smoke the drug, thus eliminating the stigma of "shooting up." Still, many users gravitate back to needles because they are the most efficient and cost-effective method of ingesting heroin.

Of course, some musicians turn to heroin precisely because it's dangerous and fits in with rock's rebellious image. That's also why many young people turn to it. For the most part, today's teens haven't seen heroin's ravages up close and personal. Anti-drug groups have dubbed it "a generational forgetting," noting that while 85 percent of those over 45 recognize heroin's terrible risks, only 50 percent of those ages 12–17 sense the danger. Burdened with a false sense of immortality, those who do turn to heroin see it as a way to defy both authority and the odds, just as they do by engaging in unprotected sex.

And there's always the "sheer stupidity" factor.

Just a few days after Jonathan Melvoin died, singer Philip Anselmo of the metal band Pantera was briefly unconscious after overdosing on heroin before being revived. Anselmo was decidedly unrepentant, instead bragging to the media about being dead for five minutes and insisting he wasn't a junkie, but an IV-abuser. He apparently experienced no great insights in the nether world.

Tyler of Aerosmith had a similar experience. Now a recovering heroin addict, he came to see himself pretty clearly:

"Originally we were musicians dabbling in drugs, and we became drug addicts dabbling in music."

The Effects of Misogynistic Lyrics

Timothy White

In 1999 a concert was held to commemorate the thir-
tieth anniversary of the Woodstock Festival. The
show was marked by a variety of problems, including
a riot on the last night and reports of numerous sexual assaults. In the following selection, Timothy
White, an author and the editor-in-chief of *Billboard*,
contends that the misogynistic lyrics of many of the
festival's performers encouraged the attacks on
women. According to White, lyrics cannot make
people do right or wrong, but they can encourage
their listeners to act on certain feelings. He concludes
that the media need to report on the problem of violent lyrics and not let such songs be treated as a joke.

"INTENT" IS DEFINED AS THE OPERATIVE STATE OF
mind and sense of purpose at the time of an action. As Woodstock '99 and its sad aftermath make plain, we have a serious
disconnect in the music industry in terms of owning up to in-
tentions after their consequences. The original '69 Woodstock
on Max Yasgur's New York farm was an entrepreneurial feat
that became a tribal rite, unforeseen in its size and fragile in its
virtues. Two later attempts to capitalize on the phenomenon
recast the musical lures while marketing the tribal magnetism.

As the violence and rapes marring the '99 event became
known, organizers countered that "the music was amazing,
and that's what we were there for." Actually, some of the performances seemed most amazing for their callous insensitivity

■

to human worth and safety. Moreover, Woodstock fans have always been there for its oft-touted "peace"-ful vibes as much as the merit of the artists' performances. While denouncing the violence, festival officials said the level of crime at Woodstock '99 was not inconsistent with what occurs in any population of 200,000. Yet when another New York-area event drawing some 200,000 fans took place in New York's Central Park 26 summers ago—a free '73 Carole King concert—the music was also lauded, but its only stunning aftershock emerged in a letter the deputy parks commissioner sent the *New York Times* to say how moved he was that King's fans had cleaned up so well that they saved his staff many costly hours of overtime.

The Effects of Music

Times have inevitably changed, yet it's pretty tough in any era to achieve consensus on what true transcendence is, especially now, when nobody will concede that people are responsible for each other's well-being or that music can have any appreciable effect, for good or ill, on humanity. In an industry where one noted lobbyist asserted that "music cannot cause action"—refuting a fact accepted since the dawn of civilization that music at least makes people dance—it's clear that corporate-level accountability is hard to come by.

People wonder if music makes people do right or wrong. Well, do love songs make people fall in love? Not in any simplistic sense. But when conditions are right, love songs often encourage listeners to act on such feelings. Moreover, they can prompt listeners to return to those sensitized states of mind with the aim of more loving gestures, each tender act building upon and reinforcing the other—often across a lifetime. As evidence, we have every private sentiment or public act of courtship ever venerated by the fine arts, literature, theater, dance, or cinema.

Unfortunately hate songs have an equal yet opposite impact, their extreme enmity encouraging listeners to act on fixed, latent, or emerging feelings. When a culture sanctions or celebrates hate songs, as well as the publicly degrading gestures that complement them, that culture is fostering an antihuman force doomed to flower into racism or sexual bigotry and the explosive violence they engender—whether in domestic abuse, torture, murder, rape, or mass violence.

Sexual Violence at Woodstock

Articles have described the violence toward women at Woodstock '99 as sexism—i.e., attitudes and conditions promoting stereotyping and discrimination. This characterization is too tame. What's actually on the rise in popular music, as manifested at Woodstock, is misogyny—the hateful objectification of women as sexual toys and disposable human furniture. To rape and forcibly molest doesn't show a prejudiced sexual attitude; it shows psychopathic sexual contempt.

Current wisdom maintains that the sexual violence came near the end of Woodstock '99, but *Time* quoted Jessup, Maryland, rehabilitation counselor David Schneider as witnessing an incident during Korn's set on the first night of the three-day fest in which "a very skinny girl, maybe 90 or 100 pounds" got pushed into the mosh pit, where "a couple of guys started taking her clothes off. . . . They pulled her pants down, and they were violating her." Schneider said he saw other women raped during Woodstock '99, and the crowd seemed to cheer on the offenders: "No one I saw tried to go in and rescue them."

Post-Woodstock '99 music overviews were typified by a *Boston Globe* dispatch on Limp Bizkit that praised it for "crafting a blueprint for popular music" with "knuckleheaded charmers like 'Nookie' and 'Break Stuff.'. . . Not too bad for a bunch of guys who did it all for the nookie." MTV's Kurt Loder, whose TV crew had to evacuate its chaos-engulfed base onstage during the Bizkit stint, saw things differently. "I thought the Limp Bizkit performance was pushing a lot of cheap buttons and was the most reprehensible thing I had seen," Loder told *USA Today* afterward, noting that a reciprocal lack of order in the area fed on itself. "It was just the situation. If you treat people like animals, they'll act like animals." Indeed, the *New York Times* reported that one woman was believed raped in the mosh pit as Limp Bizkit played.

Capt. John Wood of the New York State Police said some of the festival's alleged rapes were thought to have occurred on its 260-acre campsite. As the *Boston Globe* quoted attendee Elizabeth Chanley, "It was a 'Lord Of The Flies' situation in the campground."

The crude degradation of women in the music of Limp

Bizkit, kindred Woodstock '99 cohorts, or colleagues like Eminem (who gets "love and respect" in the credits of Bizkit's new "Significant Other" album) is often dismissed as harmless "limit-pushing" for hard-partying fans. Yet what's most cruel and self-perpetuating about date or party rape—according to agencies helping victims of sexual abuse—is precisely that it's commonly treated as a joke when men drug young women, when they violate those unconscious/defenseless women, and when weeks later they brag about the assaults while blaring hit records extolling the joys of party-raping and butchering women.

Ignoring the Issues

The music press often avoids reporting on these issues. After an August Lilith Fair press conference in Boston where Sheryl Crow commented on Lilith's sharp contrast with Woodstock '99, a Lilith organizer said the conference was the first at which the press inquired about Lilith's dollar-a-ticket donations to local women's charities. In Boston, the funds went to Respond Inc., the organization helping battered women and children that also issued the acclaimed "Respond" benefit CD. For *Billboard*'s part, when this columnist suggested last March that readers buy the "Respond" album instead of Eminem's "The Slim Shady LP"—the latter an instrument of self-confessed misogyny intended (by an artist who now concedes he needs psychotherapy) to target the estranged mother of his infant daughter, plus his own mom—none of dozens of articles citing this writer's criticisms of Eminem mentioned that half of that column was devoted to the "Respond" CD and the desperately needed aid it supports.

By the way, Carole King's serene '73 Central Park concert marked the debut of her hit "Believe In Humanity"; its finale was "You've Got A Friend." Then, as now, the feelings that an artist offers an audience are usually reciprocated.

Offensive Lyrics Should Be Criticized, Not Censored

Sam Brownback

In the following selection, Kansas senator Sam Brownback explains his views on violent and degrading lyrics. Brownback argues that censorship is inappropriate in a free society. However, Brownback contends, while all speech should be permitted, certain forms should not be considered respectable. He maintains that lyrics glorifying murder, rape, and other crimes are dangerous because they will lead to a more violent society. Brownback concludes that such songs should be publicly evaluated and criticized. This speech was originally given to the City Club in Cleveland on March 23, 1998.

I WANT TO TALK WITH YOU TODAY ABOUT MUSIC and freedom about lyrics, liberty and license. This is an issue that is important to me—as it is, I suspect, important to you. I can't think of a more fitting place for this discussion here, at a forum dedicated to upholding the principle of free speech, in Cleveland, the home of the Rock and Roll Hall of Fame.

As many of you know, I held a Senate hearing on the impact of violent music lyrics on young people. During this hearing, we heard a variety of witnesses testify on the effects of music lyrics that glorified rape, sexual torture, violence and

■

Reprinted, with permission, from "Free Speech: Lyrics, Liberty, and License," a speech by Sam Brownback delivered to the City Club of Cleveland, Ohio, March 23, 1998.

murder. Some of these lyrics are almost unbelievably awful but they are backed by huge, powerful, prestigious corporations. I have grown more and more concerned about the content and the impact of these lyrics. And I have publicly criticized the entertainment executives who produce, promote, and profit from such music.

Two Mistaken Views

I am also the only Senator on the Commerce Committee to vote against a very popular bill that would coerce TV stations into labeling their programs.

I publicly opposed V-chip legislation. [The V-chip is technology that enables parents to block television shows they do not want their children to see.] I have consistently voted against any sort of government involvement in regulating or rating music or television.

Some people don't think the two go together. They think that if you talk about some music lyrics being degrading and violent, then you must be in favor of censorship. Others think that if you vote against various government restrictions on television programs, or music content, you must approve of those programs and songs. Both views are mistaken.

And today, I'd like to talk about legislating in a way to maximize freedom, and agitating for civility and decency, and why the two not only can go together, but should—and indeed, if we are to preserve freedom, they must.

The Consequences of Music

Most of you here have strong ideas about music. As indeed, you should. Music is powerful. It changes our mood, shapes our experience, affects our thoughts, alters our pulse, touches our lives. The rhythm, the beat, and the lyrics all impress us with their message. Thousands of years ago, the great philosopher Plato stated, "Musical training is a more potent instrument than any other, because rhythm and harmony find their way into the inward places of the soul, on which they mightily fasten."

As such, music lyrics have profound public consequences. In many ways, the music industry is more influential than anything than happens in Washington. After all, most people spend a lot more time listening to music than watching C-

Span or reading the newspaper. They're more likely to recognize musicians than Supreme Court Justices. Most of us spend more time thinking about music than laws, bills, and policies. And that's probably a good thing.

And as many of you know, no one spends more time listening to music than young people. In fact, one study conducted by the Carnegie Foundation concluded that the average teenager listens to music around four hours a day. In contrast, less than an hour is spent on homework or reading, less than 20 minutes a day is spent talking with Mom, and less than five minutes is spent talking with Dad. If this is true, there are a lot of people who spend more time listening to shock-rock artist Marilyn Manson or Snoop Doggy Dogg than Mom or Dad. In fact, Marilyn Manson himself said: "Music is such a powerful medium now. The kids don't even know who the President is, but they know what's on MTV. I think if anyone like Hitler or Mussolini were alive now, they would have to be rock stars."

In short, because of the power of music, the time we spend listening to it, and the potency of its messages, music has a powerful public impact. It affects us, not only privately, but publicly. It helps shape our attitudes and assumptions, and thus, our decisions and behavior—all of which has a public dimension, and merits public debate.

Frankly, I believe there needs to be more public discourse over music. It is too important to ignore. Its influence reaches around the world. American rock and rap are popular exports. They are listened to by billions, in virtually every nation on earth. And for good or bad, our music shapes the way in which many people around the world view the U.S.—American music is the most pervasive (and loudest) ambassador we have. Unfortunately, its message is too often a destructive one.

Offensive Lyrics Are Becoming Popular

Over the past few years, I have grown concerned about the popularity of some lyrics—lyrics which glorify violence and debase women. Some recent best-selling albums have included graphic descriptions of murder, torture, and rape. Women are objectified, often in the most obscene and degrading ways. Songs such as Prodigy's single "Smack My Bitch Up" or "Don't Trust a

Bitch" by the group "'Mo Thugs" encourage animosity and even violence towards women. The alternative group Nine Inch Nails enjoyed both critical and commercial success with their song "Big Man with a Gun" which describes forcing a woman into oral sex and shooting her in the head at pointblank range.

Shock-rock bands such as "Marilyn Manson" or "Cannibal Corpse" go even further, with lyrics describing violence, rape, and torture. Consider just a few song titles by the group "Cannibal Corpse"; "Orgasm by Torture", or "Stripped, Raped and Strangled." As their titles indicate, the lyrics to these songs celebrate hideous crimes against women.

Many of you may already know the kind of lyrics I am talking about. If not, it is useful to read some of them—they won't be hard to find; they are quite popular. Then ask yourself: what are the real-world effects of these lyrics? What do these lyrics celebrate, and what do they ridicule or denounce? What are the consequences of glorifying violence and glamorizing rape? Have record companies behaved responsibly when they produce music that debases women? You and your friends may come up with different answers. But they are good questions to think about. And I hope recording industry executives think about them as well.

It is a simple fact of human nature that what we hear and see, what we experience, affects our thoughts, our emotions, and our behavior. If it did not, commercials wouldn't exist, and anyone who ever spent a dollar on advertising would be a complete fool. But advertising is a multibillion dollar business because it works. It creates an appetite for things we don't need, it motivates us to buy things we may not have otherwise. What we see and hear changes how we act.

Debating the Issue

Now think back to the music we have been talking about. How do these lyrics affect their fans? Different people will be affected different ways. Some teens are more vulnerable than others. Young people who grow up in strong families, going to good schools, with adults who are committed to them, are probably going to be just fine. But let's consider what happens in some of America's inner cities, where many young men grow up without fathers, without good schools, surrounded by violence—how does this affect the way they think about, and treat women? Moreover, there have already been several studies done that have pointed to a loss of self-esteem among girls and young women. How does the fact that some of the best-selling albums feature songs that refer to them exclusively as "those bitches and sluts" affect them?

There are no easy answers to those questions. It is impossible to quantify the ways in which such lyrics affect us. But it is equally impossible to believe they have no effect at all.

Of course, most rock and rap do not have hyperviolent or perverse lyrics. In the grand scale of things, it is a small number of songs from an even smaller number of bands that produce these sort of lyrics. They are the exception, not the rule.

It is also true that people will disagree over which music is offensive. Some people thought the Beach Boys were a problem, and some think the Spice Girls are. I do not happen to be one of them. There will always be songs about which reasonable people with good judgement will disagree.

But there should also be some things that we can all agree upon. And one of those things is that music which glorifies rape, violence and bigotry is wrong. It may be constitutionally protected. The huge entertainment corporations that produce, promote and profit from this sort of record may have a right to do so. But it is not the right thing to do.

A Senate Hearing

So [in November 1997], I held a hearing on the impact of music lyrics which glorified violence and debased women. We heard from a variety of witnesses—a parent, a representative from the American Academy of Pediatrics, a Stanford Professor, the head of the Recording Industry Association, and the head of the National Political Congress of Black Women, who has campaigned against gangsta rap. Should any of you want to see the record of the hearing, you may do so by logging on to my senate web site.

I held this hearing for two reasons: 1) to raise public awareness of some of these lyrics, so that potential consumers can make more informed judgements before they buy the music, 2) to examine, through hearing from witnesses from the medical and academic communities, the impact of such lyrics on youth attitudes and well-being.

It is a particularly important time to do so. Actual and virtual violence have dramatically increased over the last few decades. Over the last thirty years, violent juvenile crime has jumped over 500%. Teen suicide has tripled.

Crimes against women have increased. Casual teen drug use has jumped by almost 50 percent in the last four years alone.

There is also a sense that we have lost ground in ways that defy easy measurement. There is a feeling that we as a society have grown coarser, meaner, more alienated. Violence seems not only more widespread but less shocking. We have become more accustomed, and more tolerant, of tragedy, violence, and hate.

At the same time, there has been a marked increase in violence and misogyny in popular music. Now, this is not to say that music violence was the cause of real-life violence. Music is only one slice of the entertainment world, a small part of the popular culture. Whatever impact music has on our attitudes and behavior is bound to be complex and variant. But the best way, I believe—then and now—to determine what that impact is, what influence violent lyrics exert, is to encourage research, debate and discussion.

During the hearing, we did not call for censorship. We did not propose, consider, or tolerate any restriction of free speech. We did not ask for legislation, regulation, litigation or any other machination of government that would prohibit even the most racist, violent, antiwoman lyrics. When it comes to First Amendment issues, I vote as a libertarian. I have voted against labels, against restrictions, against government meddling. But it is not enough to merely legislate in a manner to protect freedom. It is also necessary to agitate for the cultural conditions that safeguard freedom. Let me explain what I mean.

Criticism Instead of Censorship

For free societies to endure, there must be a distinction between what is allowed and what is honored. I believe that the First Amendment assures the widest possible latitude in allowing various forms of speech—including offensive, obnoxious speech. But the fact that certain forms of speech should be allowed does not mean that they should be honored, or given respectability. There are many forms of speech that should be thoroughly criticized, even as they are protected. Freedom of expression is not immunity from criticism.

The proper response to offensive speech is criticism—not censorship, and not apathy. Vigorous criticism of the perverse, hateful, and violent reflects a willingness on the part of citizens to take ideas seriously, evaluate them accordingly, and engage them directly. A cultural predisposition to care about ideas and to judge between them—while protecting the liberty of others—is the best bulwark of a free society. A citizenry that evaluates ideas, that discerns the true from the false, that values reason over reaction, that affirms that which is edifying, and that refutes that which is wrong—is exactly the society most likely to value, to have, and to keep free speech.

What we honor says as much about our national character as what we allow. There is an old saying "Tell me what you love, and I'll tell you who you are." The same can be said of societies, as well as individuals. What we honor and esteem as a people both reflects and affects our culture. We grow to resemble what we honor, we become less like what we disparage. What we choose to honor, then, forecasts our cultural condition.

This is important, because there are cultural conditions which make democracy possible, markets open, and societies free. Democracy cannot endure in a society that has lost respect for the law or an interest in self-government. Societies become less free when they become more violent. The more culturally chaotic we become, the more restrictions, laws and regulations are imposed to maintain order.

Glorifying violence in popular music is dangerous—because a society that glorifies violence will grow more violent. Similarly, when we refuse to criticize music that debases women, we send the message that treating women as chattel is not something to be upset about. Record companies that promote violent music implicitly push the idea that more people should listen to, purchase, and enjoy the sounds of slaughter. When MTV named Marilyn Manson the "best new artist of the year" [in 1997], they held Manson up as an example to be aspired to and emulated. Promoting violence as entertainment corrodes our nation from within.

This is not a new idea. Virtually all of the Founding Fathers agreed—even assumed—that nations rise and fall based on what they honor and what they discourage. Samuel Adams, an outspoken free speech advocate, said the following: "A general dissolution of principles and manners will more surely overthrow the liberties of America than the whole force of the common enemy."

Unfortunately, in many circles, liberty is being redefined as "license"—the idea that anything goes, that all speech is morally equivalent. According to this view, we cannot judge or criticize speech—no matter how offensive we may find it. After all, what is offensive to one person, the reasoning goes, may be acceptable, even enjoyable to someone else. Thus, the idea of honoring certain forms of speech and stigmatizing others becomes seen as infringements on liberty. This assumes that to have freedom of speech, you can't give a rip over what is said—and that tolerance is achieved by apathy. Their motto can be summed up in one word: "whatever."

This is dead wrong. A philosophy of "whatever" is poison to the body politic. Civility, decency, courtesy, compassion, and respect should not be matters of indifference to us. We should care about these things—care about them deeply. We should allow both honorable and offensive forms of speech. But just as certainly, we should honor that which is honorable, and criticize that which is not. If we, as a society, come to the place where we think anything goes, the first thing to go will be freedom.

The great southern author Walker Percy once stated that his greatest fear for our future was that of "seeing America, with all of its great strength and beauty and freedom . . . gradually subside into decay through default and be defeated . . . from within by weariness, boredom, cynicism, greed and in the end, helplessness before its great problems."

A Bright Future

I am optimistic about our future, but his point is an important one. America is at a place in history where our great enemies have been defeated.

Communism—with all of its shackles on the human spirit—has fallen. The Cold War is over. Our economy is strong; our incomes up, our expectations high. We are, in a sense, the only remaining world superpower.

Certainly, the future looks bright. But our continued success is not a historical certainty. It will be determined by the character of our nation—by the condition of our culture as much as our economy, or our policies. What we value, and what we disparage, are good predictors of what we soon shall be.

This is why I have both legislated in a libertarian manner, and agitated against hateful, racist, violent music lyrics. For those of us who are concerned about the loss of civility in society, and the glorification of hate, violence and misogyny in popular music, our goal must be not to coerce, but to persuade. We should aim to change hearts and minds, rather than laws. Analyzing, evaluating, and sometimes criticizing lyrics is not only compatible with, but essential to, liberty.

May rock roll on, and freedom ring.

Albums Should Not Be Labeled

Frank Zappa

In May 1985, a group of prominent Washington wives founded the Parents Music Resource Center in response to what they felt was the growing problem of indecent lyrics in popular music. The PMRC urged the record industry to regulate the content of their albums; by August 1985 the industry had agreed to place labels on albums that contained explicit lyrics. However, the PMRC sought additional steps, including the printing of lyrics on the back of the albums and a more detailed ratings system. On September 19, 1985, the Senate Commerce Committee held a hearing on pornographic lyrics in rock music, in which members of the PMRC testified.

Several musicians also testified at that hearing. One of the witnesses was Frank Zappa, known for his work as a solo artist and with the Mothers of Invention. In his testimony, excerpted here, Zappa contended that the PMRC's efforts were riddled with double standards—for example, only rock music was targeted, not any other genre—and could lead to increasing censorship. According to Zappa, parents can prevent their children from buying offensive music if they so choose. He also alleged that the record industry was willing to work with the PMRC because record companies would benefit from a law, H.R. 2911, that taxed blank cassette tapes. In the end, the record industry did not agree to the PMRC's suggestions but a compromise was reached on warning stickers.

■

From Frank Zappa's testimony before the U.S. Senate Committee on Commerce, Science, and Transportation, September 19, 1985.

THESE ARE MY PERSONAL OBSERVATIONS AND opinions. They are addressed to the Parents Music Resource Center (PMRC) as well as this committee. I speak on behalf of no group or professional organization.

The PMRC proposal is an ill-conceived piece of nonsense which fails to deliver any real benefits to children, infringes the civil liberties of people who are not children, and promises to keep the courts busy for years, dealing with the interpretational and enforcemental problems inherent in the proposal's design.

It is my understanding that, in law, First Amendment Issues are decided with a preference for the least restrictive alternative. In this context, the PMRC's demands are the equivalent of treating dandruff by decapitation.

A Suspicious Bill

No one has forced Mrs. Baker or Mrs. Gore to bring Prince or Sheena Easton into their homes. Thanks to the Constitution, they are free to buy other forms of music for their children. Apparently they insist on purchasing the works of contemporary recording artists in order to support a personal illusion of aerobic sophistication. Ladies, please be advised: the $8.98 purchase price does not entitle you to a kiss on the foot from the composer or performer in exchange for a spin on the family Victrola. Taken as a whole, the complete list of PMRC demands reads like an instruction manual for some sinister kind of "toilet training program" to house-break all composers and performers because of the lyrics of a few. Ladies, how dare you?

The ladies' shame must be shared by the bosses at the major labels who, through the Recording Industry Association of America (RIAA), chose to bargain away the rights of composers, performers, and retailers in order to pass H.R. 2911, The Blank Tape Tax: A private tax, levied by an industry on consumers, for the benefit of a select group within that industry. Is this a "consumer issue"? You bet it is. PMRC spokesperson, Kandy Stroud, announced to millions of fascinated viewers on [an] ABC Nightline debate that Senator Al Gore, a man she described as "A friend of the music industry," is co-sponsor of something she referred to as "anti-piracy legislation". Is this the same tax bill with a nicer name?

The major record labels need to have H.R. 2911 whiz through a few committees before anybody smells a rat. One of them is chaired by Senator Thurmond. Is it a coincidence that Mrs. Thurmond is affiliated with the PMRC? I can't say she's a member, because the PMRC has no members. Their secretary told me on the phone that the PMRC has no members . . . only founders. I asked how many other D.C. wives are nonmembers of an organization that raises money by mail, has a tax-exempt status, and seems intent on running the Constitution of the United States through the family paper-shredder. I asked her if it was a cult. Finally, she said she couldn't give me an answer and that she had to call their lawyer.

While the wife of the Secretary of the Treasury recites "Gonna drive my love inside you . . . ," and Senator Gore's wife talks about "Bondage!" and "oral sex at gunpoint," on the CBS Evening News, people in high places work on a tax bill that is so ridiculous, the only way to sneak it through is to keep the public's mind on something else: 'Porn Rock'.

The PMRC practices a curious double standard with these fervent recitations. Thanks to them, helpless young children all over America get to hear about oral sex at gunpoint on network TV several nights a week. Is there a secret Federal Communications Commission (FCC) dispensation here? What sort of end justifies THESE means? PTA parents should keep an eye on these ladies if that's their idea of 'good taste'.

Is the basic issue morality? Is it mental health? Is it an issue at all? The PMRC has created a lot of confusion with improper comparisons between song lyrics, videos, record packaging, radio broadcasting, and live performances. These are all different mediums, and the people who work in them have a right to conduct their business without trade-restraining legislation, whipped up like an instant pudding by The Wives of Big Brother.

Is it proper that the husband of PMRC non-member/founder/person sits on any committee considering business pertaining to the Blank Tape Tax or his wife's lobbying organization? Can any committee thus constituted 'find facts' in a fair and unbiased manner? This committee has three. A minor conflict of interest?

The PMRC promotes their program as a harmless type of

consumer information service providing 'guidelines' which will assist baffled parents in the determination of the 'suitability' of records listened to by 'very young children'. The methods they propose have several unfortunate side effects, not the least of which is the reduction of all American Music, recorded and live, to the intellectual level of a Saturday morning cartoon show.

Teen-agers with $8.98 in their pocket might go into a record store alone, but 'very young children' do not. Usually there is a parent in attendance. The $8.98 is in the parents pocket. The parent can always suggest that the $8.98 be spent on a book.

Reasons for and Approaches to Censorship

Rock 'n' roll and rap music have become the blame for what was wrong with the country's emerging adults. Popular music that not only sounds different but has suggestive lyrics aimed at children frightens many parents. The response has been a series of attempted controls that have encompassed government as well as economic and commercial forms of censorship.

The justification for such controls is based on fears about the effects of rock and rap words and music: that such expressions might cause youth to become ungovernable, unlikely to follow society's rules. The possible effects include modeling of bizarre behavior, as well as imitating alien sounds, speaking taboo words, emulating violent lyrics, fulfilling sexual desires, copying the performers' outlandish antics and being overwhelmed by extreme audience reactions. Many adults see the musicians as instigators, whose compositions and actions violate society's norms and appear to encourage sexual antics and savagery such as murder, drug use and suicide. Because music can convey feelings and emotions, the danger of this music is clear and present to those who fear these behaviors, and

If the parent is afraid to let the child read a book, perhaps the $8.98 can be spent on recordings of instrumental music. Why not bring jazz or classical music into your home instead of Blackie Lawless or Madonna? Great music with no words at all is available to anyone with sense enough to look beyond this week's platinum-selling fashion plate.

Children in the 'vulnerable' age bracket have a natural love for music. If, as a parent, you believe they should be exposed to something more uplifting than sugar walls, support Music Appreciation programs in schools. Why haven't you considered your child's need for consumer information? Music Appreciation costs very little compared to sports expenditures.

fear it enough to justify censorship and control. . . .

Censoring music can be indirect. Consumers have been urged to boycott concerts and to refuse to purchase the music that parents and other adults have publicized as detrimental. Businesses and discount chain mega-stores respond to public pressures and refuse to carry the offending music, especially the music labeled obscene or violent. The industry can censor itself and chill expression, no matter how financially successful. The country's youth, as the prime consumers of new musical forms, have long purchased tapes, records and CDs, listened to radio, watched MTV and attended concerts. Rock in its many forms into Rap topped the musical purchases by dollar value. Industry executives, Time-Warner for one, avoid those artists or groups who are so controversial as to hurt sales. Besides being influenced to some degree by the youths' musical preferences, music companies do react to strong parental groups who protest that particular lyrics are too violent or too sexually suggestive and obscene. And some individuals have sued musicians and music businesses because of suspected effects to them and their families.

Betty Honchin Winfield, from Betty Honchin Winfield and Sandra Davidson, eds., *Bleep!: Censoring Rock and Rap Music*, 1999.

Your children have a right to know that something besides pop music exists.

A Slippery Slope

It is unfortunate that the PMRC would rather dispense governmentally sanitized Heavy Metal Music, than something more 'uplifting'. Is this an indication of PMRC's personal taste, or just another manifestation of the low priority this administration has placed on education for The Arts in America? The answer, of course, is neither. You can't distract people from thinking about an unfair tax by talking about Music Appreciation. For that you need sex . . . and lots of it.

Because of the subjective nature of the PMRC ratings, it is impossible to guarantee that some sort of 'despised concept' won't sneak through, tucked away in new slang or the overstressed pronunciation of an otherwise innocent word. If the goal here is total verbal/moral safety, there is only one way to achieve it: watch no TV, read no books, see no movies, listen to only instrumental music, or buy no music at all.

The establishment of a rating system, voluntary or otherwise, opens the door to an endless parade of Moral Quality Control Programs based on "Things Certain Christians Don't Like". What if the next bunch of Washington Wives demands a large yellow "J" on all material written or performed by Jews, in order to save helpless children from exposure to 'concealed Zionist doctrine'?

Record ratings are frequently compared to film ratings. Apart from the quantitative difference, there is another that is more important: People who act in films are hired to 'pretend'. No matter how the film is rated, it won't hurt them personally. Since many musicians write and perform their own material and stand by it as their art (whether you like it or not), an imposed rating will stigmatize them as individuals. How long before composers and performers are told to wear a festive little PMRC arm band with their Scarlet Letter on it?

Other Genres Are Ignored

The PMRC rating system restrains trade in one specific musical field: Rock. No ratings have been requested for Comedy records or Country Music. Is there anyone in the PMRC who can differentiate infallibly between Rock and Country Music? Artists in both fields cross stylistic lines. Some artists include comedy material. If an album is part Rock, part Country, part Comedy, what sort of label would it get? Shouldn't the ladies be warning everyone that inside those Country albums with the American Flags, the big trucks, and the atomic pompadours there lurks a fascinating variety of songs about sex, violence, alcohol, and the devil, recorded in a way that lets you hear every word, sung for you by people who have been to prison and are proud of it.

If enacted, the PMRC program would have the effect of protectionist legislation for the Country Music Industry, providing more security for cowboys than it does for children. One major retail outlet has already informed the Capitol Records sales staff that it would not purchase or display an album with any kind of sticker on it.

Another chain with outlets in shopping malls has been told by the landlord that if it racked "hard-rated albums" they would lose their lease. That opens up an awful lot of shelf space for somebody. Could it be that a certain Senatorial husband and wife team from Tennessee sees this as an 'affirmative action program' to benefit the suffering multitudes in Nashville?

Keeping Children Away from Sex

Is the PMRC attempting to save future generations from SEX ITSELF? The type, the amount, and the timing of sexual information given to a child should be determined by the parents, not by people who are involved in a tax scheme cover-up.

The PMRC has concocted a Mythical Beast, and compounds the chicanery by demanding 'consumer guidelines' to keep it from inviting your children inside its sugar walls. Is the next step the adoption of a "PMRC National Legal Age For Comprehension of Vaginal Arousal". Many people in this room would gladly support such legislation, but, before they start drafting their bill, I urge them to consider these facts:

(1) There is no conclusive scientific evidence to support the claim that exposure to any form of music will cause the listener to commit a crime or damn his soul to hell.

(2) Masturbation is not illegal. If it is not illegal to do it, why should it be illegal to sing about it?

(3) No medical evidence of hairy palms, warts, or blindness has been linked to masturbation or vaginal arousal, nor has it been proven that hearing references to either topic automatically turns the listener into a social liability.

(4) Enforcement of anti-masturbatory legislation could prove costly and time consuming.

(5) There is not enough prison space to hold all the children who do it.

An Offensive Proposal

The PMRC's proposal is most offensive in its "moral tone". It seeks to enforce a set of implied religious values on its victims. Iran has a religious government. Good for them. I like having the capitol of the United States in Washington, DC, in spite of recent efforts to move it to Lynchburg, VA.

Fundamentalism is not a state religion. The PMRC's request for labels regarding sexually explicit lyrics, violence, drugs, alcohol, and especially occult content reads like a catalog of phenomena abhorrent to practitioners of that faith. How a person worships is a private matter, and should not be inflicted upon or exploited by others. Understanding the Fundamentalist leanings of this organization, I think it is fair to wonder if their rating system will eventually be extended to inform parents as to whether a musical group has homosexuals in it. Will the PMRC permit musical groups to exist, but only if gay members don't sing, and are not depicted on the album cover?

The PMRC has demanded that record companies "re-evaluate" the contracts of those groups who do things on stage that THEY find offensive. I remind the PMRC that groups are comprised of individuals. If one guy wiggles too much, does the whole band get an "X"? If the group gets dropped from the label as a result of this 're-evaluation' process, do the other guys in the group who weren't wiggling get to sue the guy who wiggled because he ruined their careers? Do the founders of this tax-exempt organization with no members plan to indemnify record companies for any losses incurred from unfavorably decided breach of contract suits, or is there a PMRC secret agent in the Justice Department?

Should individual musicians be rated? If so, who is qualified to determine if the guitar player is an "X", the vocalist is a "D/A" or the drummer is a "V". If the bass player (or his Senator) belongs to a religious group that dances around with poisonous snakes, does he get an "O"? What if he has an earring in one ear, wears an Italian Horn around his neck, sings about his astrological sign, practices yoga, reads the Quaballah, or owns a rosary? Will his "occult content" rating go into an old CoIntelPro computer, emerging later as a "fact", to determine if he qualifies for a home-owner loan? Will they tell you this is necessary to protect the folks next door from the possibility of 'devil-worship' lyrics creeping through the wall?

What hazards await the unfortunate retailer who accidentally sells an "O" rated record to somebody's little Johnny? Nobody in Washington seemed to care when Christian Terrorists bombed abortion clinics in the name of Jesus. Will you care when the "friends of the wives of big brother" blow up the shopping mall?

The PMRC wants ratings to start as of the date of their enactment. That leaves the current crop of 'objectionable material' untouched. What will be the status of recordings from that Golden Era to censorship? Do they become collectors' items . . . or will another "fair and unbiased committee" order them destroyed in a public ceremony?

Bad facts make bad law, and people who write bad laws are, in my opinion, more dangerous than songwriters who celebrate sexuality. Freedom of Speech, Freedom of Religious Thought, and the Right to Due Process for composers, performers and retailers are imperiled if the PMRC and the major labels consummate this nasty bargain. Are we expected to give up Article One so the big guys can collect an extra dollar on every blank tape and 10 to 25% on tape recorders? What's going on here? Do WE get to vote on this tax? There's an awful lot of smoke pouring out of the legislative machinery used by the PMRC to inflate this issue. Try not to inhale it. Those responsible for the vandalism should pay for the damage by voluntarily rating themselves. If they refuse, perhaps the voters could assist in awarding the Congressional "X", the Congressional "D/A" , the Congressional "V", and the Congressional "O". Just like the ladies say: these ratings are necessary to protect our children. I hope it's not too late to put them where they really belong.

The Myth of Satanism in Heavy Metal

Deena Weinstein

In the following selection, Deena Weinstein refutes the claim that heavy metal supports satanism. Critics of metal have long alleged that satanic messages can be found in the lyrics of the songs. Weinstein argues that these lyrics are not a religious statement but are instead critiques of a judgmental society. She asserts that cultural conservatives are threatened by heavy metal because the music offers an alternative to the white male audience that fundamentalists target.

Weinstein is a professor of sociology at DePaul University in Chicago and a reviewer of metal music. In addition to her own books, which include *Heavy Metal: A Cultural Sociology*, the source of the following viewpoint, and *Serious Rock: The Artistic Vision of Modern Society in Pink Floyd, Rush, and Bruce Springsteen*, Weinstein's essays have been published in several anthologies, including *American Popular Music: Readings from the Popular Press* and *Adolescents and Their Music: If It's Too Loud, You're Too Old*.

FROM THE VIEWPOINT OF THE FUNDAMENTALIST right wing, the most offensive and ominous characteristic of heavy metal is its supposed promotion of satanism. "Satan has gotten a real foothold in rock," asserts Richard Peck in his fundamentalist diatribe [*Rock Rock Rock: Making Musical Choices*]

■

against the music. Peck further argues that "Whenever possible Satan will use this dark side of rock to lead Christians into sin." Dr. [Paul] King, the psychologist and consultant to the Parents' Music Resource Center (PMRC), finds satanism to be at the core of heavy metal: "The attraction of heavy metal music is its message that a higher power controls the world, and that power is hate—often personified by Satan." This claim is echoed by Carl Raschke, who remarks that "In rock music, the symbols and paraphernalia of hate movements, particularly Naziism, have been the staple diet of so-called metalheads for more than a decade." Phyllis Polack, a journalist who writes for heavy metal magazines, reported that the Right has accused record companies of hiring "satan-worshipping witches to put spells on albums to make sure they sell."

Seeking Satanic Messages

In *The Triumph of Vulgarity: Rock Music in the Mirror of Romanticism*, Robert Pattison maintained that "Any number of religious fundamentalists have asserted that rock is the devil's work and some, with the hearing of dogs, have discovered subliminal messages on albums by Kiss and Led Zeppelin, more often than not audible only when the records are played backward—Satan's technological adaptation of the black mass." One of the consultants for the plaintiffs in the Judas Priest trial is Wilson Bryan Key, who is a self-styled expert on satanic messages. Key has been used as a consultant in almost two dozen cases. He now specializes in heavy metal, but he also says that he has discovered "satanic or sexual messages on five-dollar bills, Howard Johnson's place mats and Ritz crackers."

The fascination with appeals to satanism that are supposedly present in backward masking or other hidden messages on records resonates with the paranoid strain in American politics. An author [Jeffrey Burton Russell] of a scholarly analysis of the devil believes that "backmasking is an unnecessary game, since the overt lyrics are often diabolical enough." The few instances of such recording trickery were done for fun and are searched for as treats by a few fans. More cynical headbangers have judged these manipulations to be pathetic commercial ploys. But the despisers of metal are convinced that they are pervasive and efficacious.

The use of symbols of the underworld in heavy metal is an essential ground for the cultural conservative's opposition to the music. Stuart Goldman, writing in the conservative *National Review*, comments that the devil, if confronted with "the average heavy-metaler, might well claim to be a relatively innocent bystander." Such critics as Goldman are updating the traditional conservative diatribe against rock music. Denisoff cites books with titles such as *Rock and Roll: The Devil's Diversion* and statements such as "rock music is the devil's masterpiece." The charges that heavy metal is satanic simply continue an old battle, but, whereas the Rolling Stones's "Sympathy for the Devil" attracted much fire because it was one of the few

Literal-Minded Interpretations

Tipper Gore, Carl Raschke, and others condemn heavy metal musicians for even mentioning the Devil, as though there were something deviant about such mysticism. Yet a 1990 Gallup Poll found that 55 percent of the American public believes in the Devil, up from 39 percent in 1978; half believe that demonic possession sometimes takes place. In light of these statistics, it is perhaps surprising that comparatively little heavy metal touches on satanic topics. But as with other transgressive icons, the Devil is used to signify and evoke in particular social contexts; he is not simply conjured up to be worshipped. Even King Diamond, heavy metal's most infamous "Satanist," is scornful of his critics' literal-mindedness: "Satan, for me, is not like the guy with two horns and a long tail. I don't believe in hell as being a place where you burn for eternity. That's not what Satan is all about. Satan stands for the powers of the unknown, and that's what I'm writing about." Heavy metal engagements with occult symbols and legends are more complex than the flat hermeneutics of the PMRC would have it.

Iron Maiden is among the most mystical and philosophical of heavy metal bands; many of their lyrics taking

songs of its time making use of satanic themes, the symbols of the underworld abound in heavy metal.

Heavy Metal Is Not Anti-Religion

To single out metal as an expression or cause of satanism is absurd on the face of it. Symbols of satan are found in nonreligious cultural forms and artifacts throughout the West, from plays and short stories to Mardi Gras and Halloween celebrations. Moreover, most of the use of the imagery of the underworld in heavy metal is underscored by a tone that ranges from irony to burlesque. In the world of metal, hell is the place where bad boys boogie, and, according to AC/DC, it "ain't a

inspiration from the Bible, Romantic poetry, and various other mythologies, explore the meaning of life, the contingency of existence, and the mysteries of fate and death. Critics often label them a "satanic" group, citing lines such as these, from "The Number of the Beast":

> The ritual has begun, Satan's work is done
> 666 the number of the beast
> Sacrifice is going on tonight

But the lines that immediately follow (less often quoted) complicate the simple endorsement read by critics:

> This can't go on, I must inform the law
> Can this still be real, or some crazy dream?
> But I feel drawn towards the evil chanting hordes

The lyrics are less concerned with celebrating satanic rituals than with exploring tensions between reality and dream, evil and power. As one fan told me, adults tend to take everything too literally, not understanding more sophisticated allegorical or figurative meanings. Just as important, criticisms of metal often emanate from those who strive to eliminate difference and ambiguity in order to enforce their own brand of morality.

Robert Walser, *Running with the Devil: Power, Gender, and Madness in Heavy Metal Music*, 1993.

bad place to be." Metal artists are less likely than members of
the general public to be true believers in the devil. For example, a member of Slayer, a band that is maligned by conservative critics, states, "I'm interested in it. . . . I'm not religious in
any way." [Richard] Corliss agrees that Slayer is not satanistic.
He compares their live shows to a Broadway musical—"*CATS*
with a nasty yowl." Metal insider Dante Bonutto, who hosts
the British Friday Rock Show, states, "I mean Slayer aren't actually in league with the devil or anything. But they do give the
impression that if they were to go to anyone's house for a
scone and a sandwich it would be his."

Heavy metal's embrace of deviltry is not a religious statement. It is a criticism of the phoney heaven of respectable society where no one boogies and everyone goes to ice cream so-
cials. It is not a countertheology. Metal lyrics do not attack
God and certainly do not malign Jesus. They just appeal to the
devil as a principle of chaos. Heavy metal is a lineal descendent
of the blues, using that style's musical and lyrical conventions.
And just as blues transformed gospel into worldly music, despair into song, and repressed sensuality into the grit of everyday life, so metal deploys Satan and suicide as symbols of freedom from and resistance against organized constraints. It is a
form of life, not of decadence.

Interviews with heavy metal artists underscore their rejection of destructive activity. In a very early (1972) article on
Ozzy Osbourne, Lester Bangs quoted his expression of revul-
sion at people slowly killing themselves with drugs. Ozzy mentioned a concert where after the show innumerable syringes
were found on the floor. "I felt sick, I really felt ill," he said
when he realized that he had just played to people who were a
"step nearer to the hole."

An Alternative to Conservative Thinking

Pattison suggests that fear of competition serves as one cause
for the misreading of heavy metal by cultural conservatives:
"Protestant fundamentalists have been quick to identify rock
as 'the Devil's diversion' because it encroaches on the emotional territory where charismatic religion does its business."
A letter published in *Hit Parader* demonstrates Pattison's
point: "Why can't you see the damage that your so-called

heavy-metal music is having on the youth of America? All the music does is preach hate and antireligious notions. If the children of America had a picture of God on their walls instead of photos of disgusting individuals like Ozzy Osbourne, our country would be in a much healthier state."

The argument that heavy metal is so despised by the fundamentalists because it competes with them for the allegiance of a segment of youth also applies to the progressives. That does not mean that heavy metal is either a religion or a political ideology, but that it is an alternative to those forms of thinking. Especially in the case of the fundamentalists, the white, male, and blue-collar core of the heavy metal subculture is a target group for recruiting. Heavy metal, by transvaluing many of the symbols of fundamentalist belief, appears to be a direct adversary. But heavy metal is not a counter-religion. It appropriates religious symbols for its own Dionysian and rebellious uses. Rather than enlist in service to interests on the left or the right, the metal audience sings "Kill the King" and "Animal (F**k Like a Beast)."

For the fundamentalists, however, heavy metal's appropriation of Christian symbols represents the very worst kind of blasphemy. They take the use of these symbols literally and are convinced that the music is a tool of the Anti-Christ. Satanism, along with suicide, sexual perversion, and mayhem form a unity in the fundamentalist mind. Suicide, for them, is the denial of God's gift of life. In terms of the belief that we are all made in God's image, killing oneself is akin to deicide. Sexual perversion makes one a citizen of the fallen world, of Sodom and Gomorrah. Violence against others and the symbolization of Satan indicate affiliation with the Anti-Christ. Yet this reading of heavy metal is not carried out in terms of metal's own code. For the metal subculture these symbols are not used to denote rebellion against God and the embrace of evil, but to signal youthful rebellion against authority. Admittedly, they do speak obliquely to that part of the Christian tradition that identifies vital power with the power of an evil world, that is, with the aspect of Christianity criticized by Friedrich Nietzsche. In a sense what heavy metal is saying is that if society chooses to place the power of ecstatic experience in the realm of evil, then I will call myself evil. Such a rhetorical move is made commonly in the culture at large. The symbol of the devil is used throughout the popular culture, in the names given to muscle cars and the names and mascots of sports teams—in other words, wherever worldly power is involved. Heavy metal's viewpoint is Dionysian and rebellious, not directly anti-Christian. Despite the few sociopathic individuals who attach themselves to heavy metal, its core appeal is to a marginalized social group whose members feel the strains of marginalization, and not to deviant or disturbed individuals.

A Coping Mechanism

The playful, not sinister, use of the term "evil" and its symbols in heavy metal is not a call to act out evil deeds, but a transvaluation of the values of respectable culture. Evil is a metonym for the proud pariah's rejection of respectable society. It is also, in part, an introjection of the respectable society's judgment of the marginalized youth, a way of both turning that judgment on the judged and against the judge. That is, the use of satanic symbols reflects the ambivalence of the proud pariah: it is a compromise formation, in Sigmund Freud's sense of that term: a way of reconciling the emotional strain between grasping the goodness of vitality and not being able to escape, within oneself, from society's judgment of one as a failure. Heavy metal is a cultural coping mechanism.

"Am I Evil?" One can introject a poor self-image or choose a strategy of transvaluing values. The strategy of transvaluation has been adopted throughout history and is present in contemporary social movements such as gay rights, feminism, and Afro-centrism. At its best it is a rebellion against inauthentic culture, an attempt of life to raise itself above the herd. In heavy metal the transvaluation of religious symbols joins with the sound of the music, which is inherently vitalizing, to tweak a devitalizing, bureaucratic, inauthentic, iron-caged, and unfair world.

EXAMINING POP CULTURE

The Future of
Rock and Roll

The Power of Major Labels Has Harmed the Development of Rock Music

Mark Crispin Miller

In the following selection, Mark Crispin Miller argues that the dominance of a handful of major record labels has made it difficult for new acts to develop. According to Miller, these labels offer multimillion dollar deals to established stars that are often past the prime of their careers instead of spending that money on unknown acts. Major labels further limit artists by only signing artists who fit a particular genre. When a new band does succeed, writes Miller, they are expected to not change their style. He concludes that musicians need to fight back against the industry's oligopoly. Miller is a professor of media studies at New York University and the director of the Project on Media Ownership, an organization that examines oligopolies in American culture.

WOULDN'T IT BE NICE IF ROCK AND ROLL WAS once a good time pure and simple—and not a cutthroat business, too? Sadly, that sweet music always had the Man behind it, counting the receipts and yelling "Shake your money-

■

maker!" At first, there were crafty profiteers like Leonard Chess, who stiffed Chuck Berry and Bo Diddley; Roulette Records' Morris Levy, whose broad influence on early rock— *Variety* dubbed him "the Octopus" in 1957—owed plenty to his mob connections; and "Col." Tom Parker, who kept as much as 50 cents out of every dollar Elvis made from the end of 1955 until his death (and after it).

But the biggest beneficiaries of pop's commercialism, finally, were no lone goniffs, but the major record companies, which really cleaned up in the sixties. Though they'd been slow to spot the gold in rock and roll (because their people hated it), the majors soon caught on, and then prevailed: Warner, CBS, PolyGram, RCA, MCA and Capitol-EMI had 81 percent of U.S. market share by 1974. (By the early eighties, the Six had also taken over distribution, driving out the many independent firms that had long supplied the record stores.) The profits were immense—high enough to lay the basis of the national entertainment state: Warner Bros. could not have gone on to become the largest media corporation in the world without that awesome income from electric blues and acid rock.

Financial Problems in the Record Industry

The Six went global in the eighties. After a calamitous post-disco crash in 1979, the industry bounced back, thanks mainly to the compact disc. As millions chucked their vinyl for the pricier CDs, the business surged again; and several media giants, hot to rock the whole wide world, came courting. Thus were the Six sucked into the transnational behemoth that now makes the whole world sing: CBS went to electronics giant Sony of Japan in 1985, then RCA went to Bertelsmann of Germany; PolyGram (owned by the Dutch electronics giant Philips) bought Chrysalis, then Virgin; and MCA (now owned by the Canadian booze giant Seagram, and renamed Universal) bought Geffen Records. And so the Warner empire (Time Warner as of 1990) was the only major U.S.-owned purveyor of the great forms of American music—rock, r&b, blues, country, jazz—while Bruce Springsteen was making product for the Japanese, and Elvis Presley had become a German asset.

Today, this international cartel is striking out—a crisis

that's the nervous buzz of all the industry, and a frequent topic in the business press. The slump began in 1994, when the rush on CDs ended. With our vinyl oldies all replaced, "sales of tried-and-true catalog titles, from Sinatra to the Stones, have dried up," *Forbes* reports. Meanwhile, the new stuff isn't selling. Sales of rock have been going down—from 46 percent of the total U.S. market in 1987 to 33 percent [in 1996]—and pop has also slipped (from 14 to 10 percent). R&b and country have each jumped a bit (to 11 and 16 percent, respectively), and rap has jumped three points (to 9 percent). Yet even that bold, booming genre may be headed for a downswing, according to some close observers. ("Hip-hop's market probably peaked in '93 or '94," says rap label manager Jeff Chang. "Nobody wants to admit it, but it's true.") In any case, overall unit sales are flat, so such slight generic increases don't make much difference.

Typically, the business is now trying to save its bacon by promoting yet another costly format: the digital versatile disc (DVD), a six-track gizmo that promises extreme fidelity—and whose coming would force us all to buy new discs and a new thing to play them on. But no high-tech fix will solve the problem, because it's not the hardware that's unpopular. There is "a general lack of enthusiasm for current product," as one Smith Barney analyst observes. The business now is so commercial it's turning people off. Quoting a recent study by two industry associations, she notes that "consumers generally perceive the music industry as 'focused on profit' and 'unoriginal.' As a result, follow-up albums that are rushed to market have received a cold reception from consumers."

Surely that big chill has many causes, some larger than the current practices within the business. First of all, rock's definitive outrageousness may finally be impossible, now that everyone has seen it all already. "To me, that's what rock and roll should always come down to—the un-allowed," says punk band manager Leee Black Childers, noting a theatrical faux-terrorism that has clearly run its course, leaving us with big bad circus acts like Marilyn Manson. More important, the rise of MTV et al. has taken some intensity out of the sound—by lessening the impact of live shows, by favoring hot bodies over talent and by forcing every tune to take a back seat to those hypnotic, easy visuals.

Artists can and do resist such deadening trends, although it's getting harder all the time—which is where the music business is to blame. Although clearly out to make big bucks, the majors of the sixties also had the sense to listen to the musical advice of their "house freaks"—hip young producers who would freely cruise the scene in search of genius that the majors might invest in for the long term. That's all over, now that the industry belongs to tone-deaf giants that want only quick returns. Thus today's "general lack of enthusiasm" is a mass response to the industry's refusal to seek out and nurture acts that might build up a loyal following. "The shortsighted, slash-and-burn policies of the '90s," writes Michael Greene in *Billboard*, "have virtually eradicated any kind of sound, coherent approach to the development of new talent." Instead, those working for the Six seek only blockbusters, just like their counterparts within the giants' book and movie units—whose output has also received "a cold reception from consumers."

On the one hand, the Six spend tons on elder stars, through mammoth "megadeals" that have yielded many duds. "Since 1991, Michael Jackson, Janet Jackson, Aerosmith, Mötley Crüe, The Artist Formerly Known as Prince, ZZ Top and the Stones have all signed megadeals," reports Keith Moerer. "Stars who sign megadeals," as he notes, "never seem to produce great albums musically," nor do such works earn out those vast advances—money that will *not* be spent on several artists just as good, and still unknown.

An Obsession with Conformity

Meanwhile, the Six are also overspending in their scramble for the Next Hot Thing—which, by the time it hits the stores, won't even be lukewarm. "EMI Records is looking for its own 'Macarena'—but with a Far Eastern flavor," began a recent article in *Billboard*. Likewise, since the relative success of Philips' Hanson, a just-pubescent trio of Nordic siblings out of Oklahoma, there's been a run on other little kids with talent; [in 1996] Ben Kweller, 16, had more than a dozen labels fighting to sign Radish, the child's band. Such "copycat signing," says *Billboard*'s Melinda Newman, is "one of the biggest problems in the industry," freezing out musicians who don't fit an image set by someone else.

A Reconfigured Industry

The music industry has been and continues to be reconfigured. The majors have become multinational media and leisure corporations no longer based on North Atlantic capital. The relations between these transfigured majors and independent record companies have become less hostile (even while it has become more difficult for the latter to survive economically) as the majors increasingly come to view the independents as their own "minor" league. At the same time, the source of profits is shifting: at the moment, it still depends heavily upon the sale of CDs, but that is largely because of the trade practices that have attempted to increase their price even while the actual cost of production decreases. On the other hand, a greater share of the profit depends on selling secondary rights across media, and on secondary merchandising. All of this is, of course, taking place in the context of the shifting distribution of the market for music across age and geography, and the changing relative importance of different media (from radio to television) for introducing new music.

Similarly, the particular media economy, the particular structured relationship between aural and visual imagery which characterized the rock formation is changing. As Tony Parsons has written:

> Pop culture [read here the rock formation], though it lives on in the hearts of those of us between the ages of 30 and 50, has largely been replaced by game culture. But any industry that still generates around [twenty-five billion dollars] worldwide every year is alive and kicking. Pop as culture is dead. Pop as industry is thriving.

Lawrence Grossberg, "Is Anybody Listening? Does Anybody Care?: On 'The State of Rock,'" from Andrew Ross and Tricia Rose, eds., *Microphone Fiends: Youth Music and Youth Culture*. New York: Routledge, 1994.

That conformist pressure has affected every genre. "Now how many women rockers do we have?" asks Georges Sulmers, owner of the independent hip-hop label Rawshack. "It's not because all these people came out of the woodwork. It's because it's like, 'Maybe we can tap into that Alanis Morissette thing!' And now we're going to see a lot more ska bands because (Seagram's) No Doubt has sold however many records." Rap too has been homogenized—as well as brutalized—by the copycat disease. It's mainly gangsta rap that the giants want, says Sulmers, "because lyrics about guns and women sell."

Thus the Six will often sign young performers not for their musicianship but because they're so derivative. That impulse is, of course, not new (Dick Clark got very rich off pallid types like Fabian and Chubby Checker), but today it drives the industry from top to bottom, Greene observes: "A&R folks [talent scouts] run in packs, desperate to sign flavor-of-the-month acts, many of whom are just learning how to tune their instruments." Even those with talent don't have too much time to rise. "Years ago, artists were given a much longer shot at making it. You're no longer guaranteed that chance," says Newman. Today, she notes, an act is lucky to be carried for a year or two, until its CD finally sells—as with Jewel, or the Gin Blossoms. Although it's striking nowadays, such a wait would not have been remarkable some thirty years ago, when your label would have stuck with you through several albums, not just one.

Product, Not Music

And if you do break through, that corporate pressure *never to be different* can be as stifling as rejection. "Once an act succeeds, their attitude is 'Don't change,'" says Sulmers of the major labels. "It halts the normal progression of what people do musically." "They had very narrow expectations of what I should do," Michelle Shocked said recently of Mercury (i.e., Philips), whom she had sued to break her contract. Even huge success does not insure artistic freedom; on the contrary. What the giants want most today is not, say, ten CDs that may each gross $12 million, but one monster album that will gross ten times as much: Michael Jackson's *Thriller*, Springsteen's *Born in the U.S.A.*, Alanis Morissette's *Jagged Little Pill* (which has to date earned $200 million for Time Warner). If it works, that strategy—called "going deep" into an album—makes a major's chiefs feel very good. ("That was a great marketing experience," Al Teller, former head of CBS Records, reminisces fondly about Springsteen's album.) But that protracted blowout, although lucrative, may stall the artist, who will now spend roughly two years dedicating all his or her energies to what Fred Goodman calls "the industry's new holy trinity: videos, touring and label promotion." That means two years of playing the same old song(s)—and then a different singer will replace you, because your follow-up will surely be a letdown (even if it sells "only," say, 7 million copies).

Such aesthetic stasis, and those inflated expectations, cannot do an artist any good; but that bad influence doesn't matter to the Six, who are no more interested in powerful songs than in good novels or hard-hitting magazines. What matters to them, rather, is the media machine itself; and so they concentrate on "product" they can stretch into as many forms as possible—soundtrack albums, cover stories, TV shows and videos, ads, T-shirts, hats, whatever. It is that synergistic strain that's turning off "consumers," who are right to think they're being hustled, and that they've heard it all before.

In prior times of pop ennui—the early fifties, the age of arena rock and disco—the independents ultimately shook things up. Such renewal is less likely now, because within the seeming universe of "independent" labels, there's a whole lotta fakin' goin' on. "There's a lot of ignorance about what's actually independent and what's not," says rock band manager and lawyer Jamie Kitman. "Often record companies that appear independent are actually funded by major labels." It may be part or total ownership that puts the majors in control—or it might be the all-important vehicle of distribution. Although there are still some true mavericks such as Profile, Rykodisc and Righteous Babe (although not Maverick, which is co-owned by Time Warner), most indies now are tiny start-ups with no audience. Disney is now the lion king of "independents," and the source not only of the merry soundtrack albums for, say, *Hercules* but also of, for example, the Suicide Machines' *Destruction by Definition*, a tight blast of suburban ska ("I don't give a shit about you stupid motherfuckers!").

The rough graphics of punk rock, and the def posturing of

gangsta rap, obscure many CDs' corporate provenance. Along with Michael Jackson, Celine Dion and Neil Diamond, Sony also brings us Rage Against the Machine ("Fuck the norm"), owns Ruthless/Relativity (Bone Thugs-n-Harmony) and Ruffhouse (the Fugees), and distributes Bag, Risky Business, Slamm Dunk, Outburst and Hard Hands. Bertelsmann—publisher of *Fitness*, *Child* and *Family Circle*, and owner of BMG Christian Music Service—also distributes Time Bomb, Deconstruction Radikal and Sick Wid It, and co-owns Bad Boy Entertainment (the Notorious B.I.G.) and Loud Records (Wu-Tang Clan).

This grand ingestion of the independents is recent corporate policy, says rock historian David Sanjek. The majors started buying up the indies in the nineties as a way to "maximize all means of generating income." A giant will now snap up whole labels rather than mere acts because such ownership permits it to exploit the songs *and* the musicians throughout its other media. Moreover, the apparent gritty "independence" is itself a salable mystique—an attitude that often replaces musical invention. Kids won't shell out for an act that doesn't seem authentic: "Your cultural capital loses credibility," as Sanjek puts it. (According to New York deejay Bobbito Garcia, owner of rap label Fondle 'Em, the giants try to imitate the raw look of the indie discs.) And so, however carefully you scan that shrink-wrapped "underground" CD—the one you bought at Borders or Sam Goody—you may not know that you've just given several dollars to a multinational that also makes HARM missiles, say, or floods the inner cities with cheap wine.

Alternatives Exist

And yet there is a world of music out there—still crazy, precious, free, sublime. Turn the radio off (to quote the title of [a] CD from ska band Reel Big Fish) and, if you go looking for them, you will find a scattered multitude of excellent musicians ready, willing and quite able to (as Little Richard shouted) rip it up—the great American expression of a spirit that no league of suits can ever quite suppress, however grimly they keep looking for more ways to make the music pay. In that spirit, and for the sake of those musicians, we should look closely, and critically, at what the Six are up to—because the music has always fought back, and has been the better for it.

Digital Distribution Will Change the Music Industry

Neil McCormick

In the following selection, Neil McCormick explains how the development of MP3 technology—which converts music into a digital file that can be downloaded onto hard drives—has led to significant changes in the music industry. The popularity of MP3s has resulted in debates on the issues of intellectual property and the role of record companies. According to McCormick, MP3s could lead to the demise of albums and shift the role of record companies from production to marketing. McCormick is a music columnist for *The Daily Telegraph*, a London newspaper.

MY FRIEND THOMAS STUBBS LIVES IN THE FUture. He describes himself as a technologist: someone whose job entails advising businesses about the possible commercial and social impact of new technological advances.

Taking Advantage of New Technologies

Thom's computer is the nerve centre of his home entertainment set-up, permanently linked to the Internet (which, of course, Thomas was playing with when most of us were still getting to grips with our first PC). He can search the Web for music that interests him (much of which is available at absolutely no cost), download songs to his hard drive in less time

■

than it would take to tear open the shrink wrapping on a new CD, and add them to the virtual jukebox that has become the store for his entire digital music collection.

While most of us are still listening to radio broadcasts, Thom prefers what might be referred to as narrowcasts, enabling him to select non-stop streams of music that appeal to his own personal taste from untold number of tiny, niche-oriented Internet-based stations.

If he hears a track he likes, he can find out what it is by simply reading the accompanying data (no more waiting for verbose, self-involved DJs to forget to tell you what you've just listened to) and add it (instantly labelled and categorised) to his jukebox. Even if the song is halfway through, it will be copied from the beginning.

He can direct his computer to play different selections of music in different rooms of his house, or seamlessly transfer tunes to a new generation of portable devices with no moving parts, enabling him to listen to his own (ever-expanding) collection whether he is out jogging or driving.

"Personal cassette players and multi-CD changers are about to join all those old turntables in the technology graveyard," says Thom. And when all recorded music is on the Internet (almost certainly within the next five years) and high-speed wireless Net connections become the norm (within the next 10) we will be well on our way to having a permanent jukebox in the sky capable of hooking listeners up to any tune, anywhere, at any time.

The Spread of MP3s

The key to this brave new digital world is a piece of freely available software cumbersomely named Moving Pictures Expert Group-1, Audio Layer 3, or MP3 for short. Essentially, MP3 compresses digital music to about a tenth of the size used for CDs by discarding all the bits of information the human ear can't hear. Well that's the theory anyway. With a good pair of headphones a discerning listener could probably tell the difference, but any discrepancies should be eradicated by the forthcoming MP4 (which uses the same technology, ensuring your brand new MP3 player won't immediately become redundant).

MP3 raged across the Internet in 1997 and 1998. Fans began

to upload their favourite CDs and trade tracks (paying little or no respect for copyright issues) while unsigned bands bypassed the mainstream recording industry by making music available on the Web. By 1999, Internet-based record companies (such as peoplesound.com), MP3 gateway sites (liquidaudio.com) and narrowcast radio stations (spinner.com) had begun to proliferate at an incredible rate. MP3 is currently the second most popular search word on the Web (the most popular also has three characters, beginning with S and ending with X).

About 846 million new CDs were sold [in 1998]. But at least six billion MP3 files were downloaded from the Net in the same period. Although a medium still in its infancy, MP3 threatens to effect the most far-reaching changes in the way we listen to, store, think about and (crucially for the music business) pay for music since Thomas Edison recorded "Mary Had a Little Lamb" onto a wax cylinder in 1877. Yet the five major record companies (Universal, BMG, Sony, EMI and Warner, who between them control more than 80 per cent of a worldwide music market worth roughly $40 billion a year) have greeted the new format like King Canute, standing at the water's edge, vainly ordering the onrushing tide to turn back.

The Financial and Legal Impact

When the first portable MP3 player was launched [in 1998] (Diamond Multimedia's Rio), the US record industry sued to stop it being sold. The judge described their case as "an exercise in futility". When that failed they set up the Secure Digital Music Initiative (SDMI) to devise a new protected technical standard for distribution of music on the Internet that they could control. Meanwhile, they made moves to try to shore up copyright protection, which is like closing the stable door after the digital horse has not only bolted but started a virtual stampede.

The protection of intellectual property is undoubtedly an important principle, but laws framed in the 18th century are being rendered almost entirely redundant by the Net's copy and distribution engines. The sheer volume of MP3 material available has given the format a kind of critical mass. All it takes is a mouse click to download every recording ever made by the Beatles, including all the band's interviews and bootlegs. It is illegal, of course, but it's free and it's easy. In belated recognition that MP3 is not going to go the same way as the eight-track cassette, the majors are . . . moving swiftly towards putting their catalogues online. . . .

Digital distribution brings into sharp focus the whole question of what a record company actually does. No longer will it be able to justify paying artists tiny royalty rates (10 per cent is common) on the grounds of the huge expense incurred putting digits on the back of plastic discs that have to pass through printing presses, be stored in warehouses and moved around on enormous fleets of trucks. All that really leaves is A&R (finding and looking after artists) and marketing and an increasing number of artists seem ready to take such matters into their own hands.

A record company might essentially be considered a filter business, but the Net by its very nature is self-filtering. There's a big smorgasbord of stuff out there, much of it complete rubbish, but new methods are rapidly evolving that channel music in dynamic, interactive ways to the consumer, with all kinds of sites and gateways and search engines configured to personal taste.

It could be boom time for the independents. The kind of marginal, artistically oriented musicians who currently struggle to survive should be able to live off earnings from a relatively small fan base, with higher royalties (Internet companies commonly offer 50 per cent or more), lower costs and the whole world to sell their product in.

Owning vs. Listening

Mind you, there are serious questions about what that product is actually likely to be. MP3 could spell the death of the long-playing album as we have come to know it. In the past 10 years compilations have outstripped the popularity of single-artist albums and, with the technology to self-select only tracks you want, consumers will be able to build up unique personal compilations. That is, if we still feel the need to own music at all.

Jim Griffin is former head of Geffen Records' New Media department and founder of consulting company OneHouse, whose clients include Microsoft and the Recording Industry Association of America. He believes that our desire to have and hold music is giving way to a simple desire to hear it.

"I think archiving almost always represents our insecurity about the efficiency of supply," he says. "Where we are assured of access to content, desire to actually have that content goes down." In other words, the virtual jukebox in the sky is about to make personal music collections redundant.

No wonder his clients don't like it when he says that their "current headaches aren't even headaches compared to what's coming".

None the less, as we accelerate into an uncertain 21st century, it would probably be a mistake to get too nervous about the future of music.

"In the Seventies, the recording industry launched a campaign to try to convince everyone that home taping was killing music," says Thom Stubbs. "Well, we all bought tape recorders. And music was still very much alive and kicking—last time I looked, anyway."

The Internet Will Not Have a Significant Impact on Rock Music

Beau Brashares

Many people have looked to the Internet as a means for changing the future of the music industry. In the following essay, Beau Brashares maintains that the Internet will have limited influence on how rock music is produced and distributed. Although record contracts can be exploitative and are weighed heavily in favor of the label, few musicians can succeed without a contract. Brashares writes that major labels continue to wield power because they know how to promote acts. Brashares has worked in the music industry and has published many articles on music, law, and technology. This viewpoint originally appeared in the briefing book for "Signal or Noise: The Future of Music on the Net," a symposium that was sponsored by the Berkman Center for Internet and Society and the Electronic Frontier Foundation.

THE INTERNET IS SUPPOSED TO KILL A LOT OF things we've gotten sick of, and give birth to better things in their places. And if there's one thing almost everybody wants to see killed and replaced, it's the music industry. We've come

■

Reprinted, with permission, from "Fifteen MB of Fame: A Music Industry Insider (and Law School Student) Gives His Perspective on How the Net Will, and Won't, Improve the Lives of Artists," by Beau Brashares, in *Signal or Noise: The Future of Music on the Net*, February 25, 2000, a briefing book published on the Internet by the Berkman Center for Internet & Society at Harvard Law School and the Electronic Frontier Foundation, at http://cyber.law.harvard.edu/events/netmusic_brbook.html.

to think of it as no more than a collection of tin-eared con-men who suck the passion out of good artists and assault us with the music of bad ones. The chorus is being swelled by almost every voice in the media and on the street:

Hey, MP3! Bring on the meritocracy of a Web-based musical marketplace, the infinite digital menu of styles and sounds, the music of the new millennium accompanied by the dying gasps of meat-space show-biz cartels.

An Exploitative Industry

Beneath the rousing din of all this revolutionary fervor, some of the parade's spectators may be asking two basic questions. One, is the traditional music business really that bad? And two, is it really going to change that much? At the risk of sounding a sour note, I'm afraid the answers are: one, oh yes; two, probably not.

Why is the record business so unpopular? To begin with, it is not exactly a free and efficient market. The mainstream music industry is controlled by a cartel of five major labels: Warner, Sony, Universal, EMI, and BMG. [In January 1999,] Warner agreed to merge with EMI, so very soon there will be only four. Over the years, these major labels have woven symbiotic relationships with related businesses that also have a limited number of players: radio, television and music retailers chief among them, but also the music press, entertainment law firms, merchandising companies, and major performance venues. These relationships form a circular web of coercive pressure that is used to atomize and disempower the artists, agents, or minor labels that don't buy in. It's a lot like professional sports was before the advent of free agency. If an athlete didn't like the lowball deal he was offered, he was welcome to try another league.

Even as these near-impenetrable networks are supposedly being threatened by new technological developments, the old-guard music business is doing just fine. It is reported to have sold 755 million units in 1999, which was 6.4% more than the previous year. But if you talk to the artists, they sound as underpaid and embittered as ever. Despite the calculated displays of glamorous excess used to market them, many of today's rock stars are essentially living on nothing but loans from their labels, and yesterday's rock stars are living by delivering pizzas. Above all, the vast majority of artists you would love to hear will never be rock stars at all. What gives?

There's a saying among musicians: before you sign a record deal, get out your dictionary and look up the word "recoupable." Recoupables have been a part of major label contracts forever, and they work like this: your band has paid its dues, generated a buzz, and potentially stands ready to reap the benefits of this work in the mainstream marketplace. A label approaches you and says, we'll spend maybe a hundred thousand on recording and releasing your record. We own the masters. You get roughly a tenth of the money we make from selling it, but all the money we spend on recording, on manufacturing, on promotion, on touring, on deli trays for the music writers is taken out of your tenth. If the record looks like a hit, the label will keep spending the band's small share on more pressing, promoting, and so on. Why not? Once the act is selling, it behooves a label to spend as much of the band's future income as possible and reap virtually all the returns. This is why a major release frequently needs to sell 500,000 copies—go gold—before sales proceeds begin reaching the band's pockets.

And while the labels lack imagination in most respects, they are notoriously creative when it comes to accounting. All in all, the deal offered to artists by a major record label is, you get the glory, and we get the money.

But what glory! The fans, the groupies, the various and sundry inebriants at one's very fingertips! How many teenagers, as they and their hormone-charged bandmates shake the shingles off their parents' garages, care about whether they will be making a living when they are 30? I know I didn't (and I'm not). Rock music has never been about amassing a sensible investment portfolio, and so long as there are young people starting bands, there will be coercive record contracts awaiting them. They'll get a slim chance at glory, while someone else will get the money.

Production and Distribution

How did such a one-sided arrangement become the norm? Well, it used to make more sense. Until recently, it was very expensive to make and sell a record, and only a well-capitalized conglomerate could afford the recording, manufacturing, distribution, and marketing of a large-scale release. With so much at risk, labels had to cover the stiffs with a heaping helping from the hits. But the circumstances that gave rise to this arrangement have been changing for a while now. For one thing, records have become a lot cheaper to record. For less than twenty grand you can buy an Alesis ADAT, a Macintosh running Digidesign's ProTools, and a Mackie mixer—the same setup used to record Alanis Morissette's monstro-smash, *Jagged Little Pill.*

Records have also become much cheaper to manufacture. Though the labels happily doubled the retail price of an album when they moved to the Compact Disc format, CDs are much cheaper to make than vinyl was. Even small-batch commercial houses that advertise in the back of music magazines will press up your CDs for 53 cents apiece.

But there's still the matter of distribution. Even as recording and manufacturing costs have come down to earth, distribution has continued to be a matter of wresting precious shelf space in street-front music stores. Since only the majors consistently have had the muscle to accomplish this with the big retail chains, even the so-called "independent" labels have had to sneak under the umbrella of the majors to reach mainstream consumers. Thus, even though a potential hit record can now be tracked and pressed by almost anyone, the major labels have maintained a hammerlock on the channels by which the product reaches the consumer.

All that's about to change, at least according to the Internet evangelists. Already, online stores like CD-Now have overcome real estate limitations, and will happily ship your obscure independent release for a reasonable fraction of the revenue. But such online retailers have so far gained only 1% of the music market, having failed to offer the drastic savings on big sellers necessary to lure more consumers from the stores. Not to worry, though, because the Internet's big gun— digital delivery of the music itself—is only starting to be aimed at the retailers. Once high-bandwidth connections become ubiquitous in the homes of consumers, music distribution will finally be free from the tyranny of brick and mortar record shops, and in turn the whole conspiracy of the record label overlords will crack like a CD jewel box. . . . Right?

Well, don't quit your day job. Bands are indeed flocking to the Internet with hopes of bypassing the major label formula for success, but so far the music-buying public is bypassing them. For example, there are 40,000 hopefuls featured on MP3.com, the biggest online aggregator of unsigned bands. Despite access to a vast audience—supposedly a half-million people visit MP3.com daily—the most successful of these web-based purveyors are selling less music online than the most dismally unsuccessful major-label acts sell at Wal-Mart. Reports are that while the free downloads are humming, MP3.com has been selling only about one CD per month for every two bands that use its service. And while that's better than nothing, the site isn't doing it for free. Besides charging a fee to be listed in their directory, MP3.com frequently requires artists to sign over all the rights to the recordings made available for download on the site, so that not a cent of publishing royalties are paid to the artist, even if the song somehow becomes a runaway smash.

But we're still waiting for that big breakthrough act to emerge from the Internet, uncompromised by the greedy major label machine. It certainly could happen, but considering that every band uploads on the hope that it will, perhaps we ought to be hearing about some of them by now.

So the Internet music revolution is not revolutionizing the balance of power just yet. Though most bands do not thrive under a traditional record deal, almost none of them survive without one. The relationship between major labels and artists still brings to mind what a down-and-out ex-boxer once said about promoter Don King: "Sure he ripped me off, but I sure wish he'd rip me off again."

The Effects of Market Saturation

What's even more worrisome for artists finding disappointment with the Internet is that, apart from some piracy-related lawsuits, the big labels haven't even seriously tried to squash it yet. When the majors finally agree on standards and get their own Internet businesses up and running, their outlook may be better than ever. They have accumulated a massive storehouse of intellectual capital, most of which will be just as good an investment in the new economy as it was in the old. One record executive, who asked not to be identified, put it this way:

> It's shocking how good labels are at what they do. . . . Every release is researched to within an inch of its life, and the level of demographic detail they have is amazing. If a rock band needs to burnish its bad-boy image, their label will tell them to start a bonfire at a music festival. It's all very calculated and its results show up in record sales. . . .

Indeed, many of today's major artists owe their success to the fact that a well-connected and well-capitalized label chose to ignore a thousand other acts and carpet-bomb the marketplace with that artist's music. Sites like MP3.com, even with their "featured artist" selections, lack this kind of filtration and emphasis, which listeners have unfortunately come to expect. It is a paradox: consumers say they want musical variety, but then they spend most freely where artistic diversity is almost non-existent. Most of them don't bother to dig for the gems even when given the chance by the Internet, keeping talented web-based artists behind the counter at the local TCBY. Meanwhile songs that could make your day or reduce you to tears simply wither on the vine, smothered by the all-out marketing assaults of Britney Spears or N'Sync.

While we're on the subject of chirpy teenaged phenomena, it is worth noting that their success has caused an army of worthy acts to accumulate at the margins of the marketplace. As the majors have worked these obscenely lucrative teen popsters, they have been systematically cutting loose the more offbeat acts that used to round out their rosters. So the offbeat bands take a chance on the Internet, because in these hard times it's all they've got. Some of them are almost getting by, particularly those who previously built a fan base with major releases. John Hall, mastermind of 80s eccentrics King Missile (remember their unlikely hit, "Detachable Penis"?), is no longer signed to Atlantic, but offers old fans new material on his website. "I sell my CDs on a webpage—they send me a check and I send them a CD. Pretty primitive." And pretty small-time, though Hall is doing a lot better than most unsigned artists online. . . .

Why Traditional Promotion Works

Why do the majors still wield such leverage, and why isn't the Internet helping, even a little, to free the long-suffering artists? There's tons of music already out there on the Net; it's already cheaper, if not free, and you don't even have to get off your ass to go to a show or a record store. What's more, everybody's tired of the old order, and there's a ton of money flowing from equity investors who want in on the new one. What do labels know that websites don't?

One thing they know is that context sells records. Internet promotion and distribution services like MP3.com, and most of the artists that use them, are underestimating the very central role of context in the pop music experience. It works like this: most of us, even if we won't fall for the commercial hype, don't like a song simply because it's inherently good. Rather, we respond to an elaborate matrix of cultural reference points that surround and inform the music. A band breaks out of obscurity because there is an elusive "something" that converges from such elements as its visual style, the impact of its stage show, and the way in which it feeds off "the scene" in its home community.

If these elements are in place, a band often can go quite far before producing a decent recording or a catchy song. That's why labels will never sign a band before attending a show in the group's hometown—they want to watch the audience. That's also why when you sign with a major label, the first order from your new bosses is: tour, tour, tour. . . .

Hope for the Internet

There are some very clever people, many of whom have launched successful acts in real space, working to make online music huge.

And they have some easy targets to start with; certain aspects of the traditional music business are looking wobbly and archaic already. Take commercial radio, for instance. It still functions as a primary music marketing device for major labels, but only because nothing better is out there yet. As John Hall predicts, "Radio as we know it will go down the toilet. There's very few stations possible, and the interests of their content providers and their advertisers are diverging so much.

The labels are trying to sell records to teenagers, and the advertisers are trying to sell cars to middle-aged commuters."

Another area where change might be due is pricing. The days of the $15 CD may be numbered, if only because developing tastes and the freedom of digital delivery will favor individual songs rather than whole albums.

"The album is kind of a 70s concept," says Joe Rosenthal, an editor at *Rolling Stone* who follows Internet music closely. "It's going to be hard to force consumers to buy a whole album in the digital format."

Indeed, the album format was largely dictated by the practical demands of manufacturing and stocking vinyl records. Those economic limitations will be disappearing, and many fans will get their songs from pirate sites unless labels allow them to buy singles at an attractive price.

Despite the continuing leverage of labels, there will also be pressure exerted on them by their top artists, who can dangle the prospect of Themself.com to get a bigger cut. "Leaving the label looks attractive when they're only giving you ten percent," says Hall. "You'd be better off selling one-ninth as many records on your own site and keeping all the money."

Following this logic, artists who have attained household-name status in the old system could be the ones who truly make out in the new one. Because while the Internet has shown little promise for developing a new act's market, it sure shows promise for selling to a market that already exists.

But major labels will be glad to modify their model here and there if there's money to be made. They will respond to pressure from consumers and established artists, but they will pass that pressure on to the artists who lack leverage, as they have always done. It's likely that all this talk of the major labels being doomed is just so much wishful thinking. And no wonder; there are a lot of wishful people out there: the ripped-off musicians, the frustrated and overcharged consumers, and most vocally, the Internet entrepreneurs who want a piece of the action.

Next time you read another article about how the Internet is certain to turn the music business upside down, reversing the positions of the historical haves and have-nots, take note of who is telling you all this. Chances are it's someone who's trying to sell you a little real estate on their hype-driven website.

Okay, so maybe the Internet isn't going to fling new stars into the skies and make a bundle for every band that deserves an audience. But maybe the revolution isn't going to be about money and fame anyhow. Every kid who starts a band isn't banking on being a rock star, and every rock star isn't in it for the big bucks and big crowds. There's all that other stuff: the joy of making noise for an audience, the rush of knowing that somewhere, people who you've never met are listening to you. It's these simple pleasures that launched a thousand garage bands, and still drive the indie-rock industry.

Rock and Roll Will Remain Relevant

James Miller

In the conclusion of his book *Flowers in the Dustbin*, James Miller evaluates the future of rock music. He observes that rock music is increasingly fragmented, making it unlikely that any future artist will have the impact of Elvis or the Beatles. In addition, the beauty of some rock songs has been countered by the increasing popularity of crude and obscene rock music. However, Miller notes that despite its flaws, rock and roll speaks to millions and will likely continue to do so. Miller is a professor of political science at the New School University in New York City.

NEARLY A QUARTER CENTURY AFTER ELVIS PRESley's death, rock and roll is as lucrative as ever: a prominent, apparently permanent feature of global culture. Without going anywhere near a living musician, one can hear the strains of various rock songs, not just on TV and in films and on the radio, but in grocery stores, in elevators, on one's telephone line while waiting to get advice on fixing one's computer. A music that once provoked the wrath of censors has become the Muzak of the Millennium.

Of course, while shopping for lettuce one is likely to hear the Beatles, and not Tupac Shakur; Whitney Houston, and not Nirvana. Some styles of rock and roll remain, by design, offensive—calculated to irritate and annoy. Gangsta rap couldn't fulfill one of its functions if its collage of beats and violent imagery failed to outrage. And the young, who enjoy

■

provoking outrage, remain the core of the music business's market: a 1991 survey of the global record industry revealed that people under the age of twenty-five accounted for well over half of total revenues.

A Fragmented Genre

Since Presley died, the world of rock and roll has become ever more fragmented, especially in the United States, where radio stations compete by delivering narrowly defined audiences to their advertisers. Genres are largely defined by the key radio formats: Top 40 (current hits no matter what style—an endangered format), urban contemporary (current dance music and romantic ballads, primarily performed by black musicians), alternative rock (music aimed largely at college students, primarily performed by white musicians, often inspired by the Velvet Underground and the Sex Pistols), hard rock (party music, aimed largely at young men, including heavy metal and grunge, invariably performed by white musicians, often inspired by the Rolling Stones), classic rock (mainly music from the Seventies and Eighties inspired by the Stones, the Beatles, and Dylan), and oldies (from the Fifties or Sixties). In addition, there are more esoteric subgenres, rarely heard on radio though often heard in clubs, for example, trip-hop and techno, synthetic cocktails of sound with a carefully calibrated number of electronically generated beats per minute.

As never before, retailers know in detail what kinds of rock actually sell, and to whom. In May 1991, *Billboard* introduced new charts based on information supplied by SoundScan, a research firm that accurately monitors sales by gathering the information from electronic cash registers that read the bar codes on albums. The new charts were revealing. The most aggressively puerile kinds of hard rock and rap sold far more than the old charts had indicated; and so did classic rock and roll recordings first issued in the Sixties and Seventies. (The charts also revealed the commercial clout of country-western, the only popular alternative to rock and roll in the Nineties, if one can really call it an alternative: the decade's most popular country artist, Garth Brooks, routinely performed classic rock songs by artists like Billy Joel and Little Feat in an energetic stage act that recalled Bruce Springsteen.)

It is unlikely that the fragmentation of the audience for pop music generally, or rock and roll specifically, will be reversed any time soon. As they always have, fans and connoisseurs reject much of what they hear. Many hard rock fans despise rap, and vice versa. Many alternative rock fans despise dance music, and vice versa. Given how deeply divided the current pop scene is, it seems highly unlikely that any future rock and roll star, however popular, will have the kind of broad cultural and social impact that Elvis had in the Fifties, or the Beatles had in the Sixties.

Michael Jackson's fate in the Eighties is symptomatic. In the two years after its release in 1982, his album *Thriller* sold some twenty-five million copies, more than any previous album in history, a record that still stands. Jackson became world-famous; but as Greil Marcus has remarked, his music asked "not to be judged by the subjective quality of the response it provoked, but to be measured by the number of objective commercial exchanges it elicited." Jackson was able to gratify his personal dream of winning renown in the *Guinness Book of World Records.* He was rich enough to become the owner of much of the Lennon-McCartney songbook, charming (or cunning) enough to wed Elvis Presley's only child, Lisa Marie. But he lacked her dad's aura of yearning spirituality— and he couldn't buy the cultural significance of the Beatles, since it wasn't for sale. One need only contrast the reception of *Thriller* to the "subjective quality of the response" to the Beatles' *Sgt. Pepper.* There is no comparison.

Reflecting on a Golden Age

In 1987, three years after the international carnival of consumption and media coverage ignited by Michael Jackson (which I witnessed firsthand, and contributed to, writing not one, but two pieces about Jackson for *Newsweek*), I was in Memphis, Tennessee. Once again, I was on assignment for *Newsweek*, this time to write about a dead white male. Gathering material for a planned cover story on the cult that had grown up around Elvis Presley in the decade after his death, I had spent several days wandering around the city, being debriefed by officials at Graceland, and interviewing Sam Phillips, among others.

One evening, I walked to a bluff overlooking the Mississippi, to watch the sunset. Since I'd grown up in the Midwest, and had spent time watching the muddy river before, I knew better than to expect a romantic panorama: but during my visit, my imagination had been fired by the idea of the blues coming up the river from New Orleans, so a romantic panorama, at least in my mind's eye, is what I was pondering.

As I pictured the musicians who had gone upriver from New Orleans to Memphis, St. Louis, and Chicago, the image of Louis Armstrong, grinning, trumpet in hand, came to mind. Armstrong, I mused, had made musical history with the Hot Five and Hot Seven in 1927, recording songs like "Potato Head Blues" and "Struttin' With Some Barbecue." Thirty years later, in 1957, Elvis Presley was making his own kind of musical history, with four consecutive number one hits: "Too Much," "All Shook Up," "(Let Me Be Your) Teddy Bear," and "Jailhouse Rock." And thirty years after that, the pop music act of the hour was an Irish "new wave" rock band, U2, at the pinnacle of its fame with songs like "With or Without You" and "I Still Haven't Found What I'm Looking For," and I was in Memphis to write about a mythic American hero.

I thought about all the musical history that had unfolded in the thirty years after 1927: an era in which jazz and the Broadway musical achieved a definitive form, and also the golden age of gospel singing, the golden age of Western swing, the golden age of Delta blues: an era associated with names like Sidney Bechet, Dock Boggs, Bing Crosby, Paul Whiteman, George Gershwin, Blind Willie Johnson, Jimmie Rodgers, Cole Porter, Fats Waller, the Boswell Sisters, Duke Ellington, Fred Astaire, Mildred Bailey, Benny Goodman, Bob Wills, Robert Johnson, Billie Holiday, Count Basie, the Soul Stirrers, Lester Young, Charlie Parker, Big Joe Turner, Rodgers and Hammerstein, Frank Sinatra, Ella Fitzgerald, Peggy Lee, Thelonious Monk, Hank Williams, Wynonie Harris, Fats Domino, Chuck Berry, Little Richard. . . .

I then thought about what had happened to American popular music in the post-Elvis era. . . .

Eschewing the balmy "moon-June" lyrics typical of an earlier era, rock and roll had introduced a refreshing realism about sexuality into popular music; it had reinforced the rhythmic complexities first made widely popular through the earlier vogues for ragtime, jazz, swing, and boogie-woogie; however imperfectly, it had irrevocably consummated the musical marriage between black and white in America, helping to bring the music of African-American performers to an audience vastly wider than anything even Louis Armstrong could have imagined. In the course of accomplishing all this, rock and roll had produced some music of stirring beauty.

But it had also produced artifacts of stunning ugliness. Punk rock had been a quintessence. Since then, most popular rock and roll acts have been musically crude or gleefully obscene or just plain silly, and sometimes (as witness highly touted albums by Marilyn Manson and the Wu-Tang Clan in the last half of the 1990s) all three at once—as if to mark the triumph of the psychopathic adolescent that Norman Mailer had warned would become the "central expression of human nature before the twentieth century is over."

For years, I had celebrated rock in print as a vibrant, triumphant hybrid of everything interesting about America's older vernacular musical traditions. But as I watched the sun set and thought about Louis Armstrong and what had come after, I was assailed with a doubt. What if rock and roll, as it had evolved from Presley to U2, had destroyed the very musical sources of its own original vitality? The music popular in America between 1927 and 1957 represented a real flowering of diverse forms. Rock and roll as represented by the Sex Pistols—or even by U2—was narrow and coarse by comparison.

I walked back to my car. Shortly after picking it up a few days before at the Memphis airport, I had discovered the radio station I would listen to for the rest of my stay. It played nothing but black church music, twenty-four hours a day. I turned on the radio and listened. Gospel music had survived. But for how much longer?

Moving Away from Criticism

By 1987, my own writing about rock for *Newsweek* had developed into a pattern: short notices of esoteric bands that struck my fancy, and longer features about celebrities, like Michael Jackson, that had struck the public's fancy. The short notices had no real meaning in the context of *Newsweek*, since the bands I fancied rarely appealed to the typical *Newsweek* reader. (I can still recall the consternation produced when I informed my editors that I wished to devote space to covering a British band called the Jesus and Mary Chain.) Meanwhile, the longer features had become an ordeal, for reasons that the British writer John Mortimer has nicely illustrated. Describing his own "quest" to secure an interview with Mick Jagger, "the middle-aged Puck," Mortimer recounted how, after an almost interminable series of delays, he was finally summoned from his hotel room with the news that Mr. Jagger was "ready to receive me in audience. I got off the bed feeling rather as Sir Galahad might have done when he was told there was someone at the front door who had come to deliver the Holy Grail, and would he please come down and sign for it."

Disenchanted by my epiphany in Memphis, and unwilling to spend the rest of my life begging for quotes from cosseted celebrities, I resolved to stop writing about rock and roll on a regular basis (though it took me several years to make good my resolution).

Of course, the history of rock and roll did not stop when I stopped writing about it, any more than it stopped after Elvis Presley died. New styles continue to come and go, some smooth, some rough, some pure, some wildly hybrid (like the London-based bhangra groups currently fusing Punjabi folk music with American Sixties funk). Since retiring from my beat, I have been happy to tune in to the rock scene casually, free of any obligation to celebrate it or dissect it, or even take it very seriously. I get a kick out of seeing my own kids get excited by new records by bands like Rage Against the Machine. And I get a kick myself out of a few newer bands. Current rock songs still color my world, and inflect the texture of my daily life.

Yes, there are other kinds of music I care for more. No, I would not wish to be stranded on a desert island with nothing but rock and roll records.

Rock and Roll Still Matters

But the fact remains that the style of syncopated dance music that Elvis Presley made globally popular (and that Louis Armstrong had helped to invent thirty years before) really is the closest thing we have to a musical lingua franca as the twentieth century ends.

Whatever its expressive limitations—and they are manifold—rock and roll speaks to millions. Out of the chaos of our time has come a prerecorded music bearing the promise of redemption through Dionysian revelry. "Tutti Frutti" and "Hound Dog" and "Lonely Teardrops" and "She Loves You" and "What's Going On" and "Born to Run" and "Anarchy in the U.K." (and, yes, "With or Without You," too) have probably touched more lives more deeply than any opera by Wagner or any symphony by Beethoven.

And because people around the world want to hear this sound, and share in the fantasies it still excites, rock and roll is here to stay—for better; for worse; and for a long time to come.

FOR FURTHER RESEARCH

Vernon Chadwick, ed., *In Search of Elvis: Music, Race, Art, Religion*. Boulder, CO: Westview Press, 1997.
  The contributors to this anthology write about their views of Elvis Presley as fans, with an emphasis on race, the South, and sexuality.

Robin Denselow, *When the Music's Over: The Story of Political Pop*. London: Faber and Faber, 1989.
  Denselow examines the political element of rock music in the United States and the rest of the world.

Paul Friedlander, *Rock and Roll: A Social History*. Boulder, CO: Westview Press, 1996.
  Friedlander chronicles the first three decades of rock and roll, emphasizing the social and historical factors that helped shape rock's different genres.

Simon Frith, *Sound Effects: Youth, Leisure, and the Politics of Rock 'n' Roll*. New York: Pantheon Books, 1981.
  In this book, Frith explores the origins of rock music and its existence as both an art form and a product.

Simon Frith and Andrew Goodwin, eds., *On Record: Rock, Pop, and the Written Word*. New York: Pantheon Books, 1990.
  Frith and Goodwin have compiled an anthology of scholarly essays on rock music that cover topics including heavy metal, the role of women, and the production and distribution of rock music.

Charlie Gillett, *Sound of the City: The Rise of Rock and Roll*. New York: Outerbridge and Dienstfrey, 1970.
  In one of the earliest analyses of rock and roll, Gillett presents an overview of the early days of the music, with a close look at the influences of blues and gospel. He also details the ways rock music changed in the 1960s, including soul music and the British Invasion.

Fred Goodman, *Mansion on the Hill: Dylan, Young, Geffen, Springsteen, and the Head-On Collision of Rock and Commerce*. New York: Times Books, 1997.
  Through a historical analysis of the careers of Bruce Springsteen, Neil Young, Bob Dylan, and their managers, Goodman traces the

development of rock and roll from a countercultural art form to a multibillion-dollar business.

David Hatch and Stephen Millward, *From Blues to Rock: An Analytical History of Pop Music*. Manchester, UK: Manchester University Press, 1987.
Hatch and Millward explore the role that blues and other African American music had in the development of rock music in America and Britain from its earliest days through the 1980s.

Greil Marcus, *Mystery Train: Images of America in Rock 'n' Roll Music*. New York: Dutton, 1982.
In one of the most famous books in rock criticism, Greil Marcus considers the role that artists ranging from Robert Johnson to Randy Newman to Elvis Presley have played in American popular culture.

Linda Martin and Kerry Segrave, *Anti-Rock: The Opposition to Rock 'n' Roll*. Hamden, CT: Archon Books, 1988.
Martin and Segrave provide a comprehensive overview of the first thirty years of censorship of rock music in America and the rest of the world, from the filming of Elvis Presley from the waist up on the *Ed Sullivan Show* to the pillorying of punk rock and disco.

Evelyn McDonnell and Ann Powers, eds., *Rock She Wrote*. New York: Delta, 1995.
Written exclusively by female musicians, scholars, and journalists, the selections in this anthology explore the female experience in rock music, from performer to fan to critic.

Legs McNeil and Gillian McCain, *Please Kill Me: The Uncensored Oral History of Punk*. New York: Grove Press, 1996.
McNeil and McCain provide a bird's-eye view into the world of punk rock in this collection that features excerpts from hundreds of interviews with the genre's figures, including Patti Smith, Joey Ramone, and Iggy Pop.

James Miller, *Flowers in the Dustbin: The Rise of Rock and Roll, 1947–1977*. New York: Simon and Schuster, 1999.
Miller traces the evolution of rock and roll in this chronological collection of essays on rock's key performers and important moments in the music's history.

Barbara O'Dair, ed., *Trouble Girls: The Rolling Stone Book of Women in Rock*. New York: Random House, 1997.

This comprehensive anthology features articles on virtually every important female artist in rock, country, jazz, rhythm and blues, and rap music as well as analyses of genres such as girl groups, female punk rockers, and riot grrrls.

Craig O'Hara, *The Philosophy of Punk: More than Noise!!* San Francisco: AK Press, 1995.
O'Hara provides a detailed explanation of the political philosophy of the punk movement. He focuses his attention on anarchism, feminism, homosexuality, and the environment.

John Orman, *The Politics of Rock Music*. Chicago: Nelson-Hall, 1984.
Orman looks into the political nature of rock music during the 1960s and 1970s, with particular emphasis on Bob Dylan, the Rolling Stones, John Lennon, and Phil Ochs. He concludes that political music lost its power in the 1970s.

Simon Reynolds and Joy Press, *The Sex Revolts: Gender, Rebellion, and Rock 'n' Roll*. Cambridge, MA: Harvard University Press, 1995.
In the first two sections of this book, Reynolds and Press examine the attitudes male rock musicians have toward women. In the final section, the authors analyze how female musicians have responded to those often-misogynistic views.

Deena Weinstein, *Heavy Metal: A Cultural Sociology*. New York: Lexington Books, 1991.
Weinstein details the development of heavy metal, analyzes its audience, and responds to critics who accuse the music of encouraging suicide and other destructive behavior.

Betty Houchin Winfield and Sandra Davidson, eds., *Bleep!: Censoring Rock and Rap Music*. Westport, CT: Greenwood Press, 1999.
Winfield and Davidson are contributors to and editors of this collection of essays on the censorship of rock and roll and rap music.

INDEX

Johnson, Robert, 11
Joplin, Janis, 103
jukeboxes, 27

Key, Wilson Bryan, 133
King, Carole, 65
King, Paul, 133
Kinks, the, 14
Kiss, 94
Kitman, Jamie, 146
Kweller, Ben, 143

Lamm, Robert, 63
Landau, Jon, 62, 64
Led Zeppelin, 16
legislation. *See* music lyrics
Lems, Kristin, 60
Lennon, John, 14
  influenced by Elvis Presley, 45–46
  singing of, 46–47
Lewis, Jerry Lee, 12, 13
Lilith Fair, 113
Limp Bizkit, 112–13
Little Richard, 12, 13
Loder, Kurt, 112
London, Herbert I., 58
LSD, 103
Lucas, Dick, 81–82
Lynyrd Skynyrd, 64

Madonna, 18
Mailer, Norman, 88, 89–90
Manson, Marilyn, 20
Marcus, Greil, 12
marijuana, 103
Marshall Tucker Band, 65
Martin, Linda, 12–13, 91
Marxism, 98
May Day demonstrations, 63
MC5, 16, 61–62
McCain, Gillian, 107
McCartney, Paul, 14, 46
McCormick, Neil, 148
McLaughlin, John, 65
McNeil, Legs, 107
Melvoin, Jonathan, 102
Michael, George, 94, 95
Midler, Bette, 65–66
Milburn, Amos, 24
Miller, James, 162
Miller, Mark Crispin, 140
Millward, Stephen, 45
misogyny, 112, 119
Mitchell, Joni, 65
Moerer, Keith, 143

Morrison, Jim, 61, 103
Mortimer, John, 167
MP3s, 148–52
MTV, 18, 142
Murcia, Billy, 104
Murray, Anne, 66
music
  and drugs, 102–103
  public influences of, 111, 115–16
  see also individual types of music
music industry. *See* record companies
music lyrics
  heavy metal, 134, 135
  labeling and regulating, 115
    focused on rock music, 128–29
    and keeping children away from
      sex, 129–30
    as offensive, 130–31
    vs. parents' choices, 126–28
    as a slippery slope, 128
    as suspicious legislation, 124–26
  violent, 114–15, 116–17
    criticism vs. censorship of, 119–22
    impact of, 117–18, 119
    Senate hearing on, 118

Nelson, Willie, 65
Newman, Melinda, 143, 145
Newport Folk Festival, 14
Newton-John, Olivia, 66
New York Dolls, the, 64
Nine Inch Nails, 117
Nirvana, 18
Nolan, Jerry, 104

Ochs, Phil, 14, 53, 55
O'Connor, Sinead, 94
O'Hara, Craig, 75
Oldham, Andrew, 15
Orman, John, 61
Osbourne, Ozzy, 16
Osgerby, Bill, 78, 79
Osmond, Marie, 66

Page, Jimmy, 16
Pareles, Jon, 16
Parents Music Resource Coalition
  (PMRC), 16, 124–31
Parker, Charlie, 103
Parson, Tony, 144
Parton, Dolly, 65
Paton, Dean, 18
Pattison, Robert, 95–97, 133, 136
Paul, Les, 12
Paxton, Tom, 55, 56